Partners in Play

Partners in PLAY

Creative Homemade Toys for Toddlers

○　❑　△　◇

Rita Anderson and Linda Neumann

An Owl Book
Henry Holt and Company
New York

Henry Holt and Company, Inc.
Publishers since 1866
115 West 18th Street
New York, New York 10011

Henry Holt® is a registered trademark
of Henry Holt and Company, Inc.

Published in Canada by Fitzhenry & Whiteside Ltd.,
195 Allstate Parkway, Markham, Ontario L3R 4T8.

Library of Congress Cataloging-in-Publication Data
Anderson, Rita.
Partners in play : creative homemade toys for toddlers /
Rita Anderson and Linda Neumann.
      p.   cm.
"An Owl book."
Includes index.
1. Toy making.   2. Play.   I. Neumann, Linda.   II. Title.
TT174.A53   1995   94-37777
745.592—dc20   CIP

ISBN 0-8050-3673-3

Henry Holt books are available for special promotions
and premiums. For details contact: Director, Special Markets.

First Owl Edition—1995

Designed by Betty Lew

Printed in the United States of America
All first editions are printed on acid-free paper.∞

1   3   5   7   9   10   8   6   4   2

The authors have made every effort to make the
information and suggestions in this book practical and workable,
but neither author assumes any responsibility for the successes, failures,
or other results of putting these ideas into practice.

To "Papa" Charles Anderson—
who made the best playthings of all

ACKNOWLEDGMENTS

The authors would like to thank *Mark Bade, Neil Schierstedt,* and *Maranatha Photography* for their contributions to this book.

CONTENTS

PREFACE

When my older son was a toddler, in 1979, I started a toddler gym and play program. I wanted to offer my son, as well as other children and parents, a variety of developmentally appropriate play experiences.

My years as an elementary school teacher taught me that a child's development must be well balanced, so I designed the play program to include a wide range of activities. I included activities to promote the development of fine motor skills (covered in this book), large motor skills, and perception skills. I incorporated activities to encourage language and sensory, social, and intellectual development. I included the parents as a major component of the play program, providing them with practical parenting information and structuring the program to make them active partners in the teaching/learning/playing experience. The program gained popularity and grew to include learn-through-play classes for infants through preschoolers.

The reaction of parents, teachers, and daycare providers to my classes and to the talks I've presented has been consistent over the years. Adults enjoy learning new ways of playing with children, and they're eager to apply my ideas. That's how this book, *Partners in Play,* came to be. It was written as a guide for adults to the kinds of materials they can use for play and ways to combine those materials to create toys and activities appropriate for one- and two-year-olds.

In writing this book, I hope to enrich playtime for children and for adults. Parents are a young child's first and best teachers, and I want to help parents recognize their potential as teachers as well as play partners. I want to emphasize that teaching your child doesn't require a degree in education or an extreme amount of time. Teaching can happen all day long with materials from around the house. To busy teachers and daycare providers, I want to offer ideas for enriching the learning environment using simple toys and activities that require a minimal investment of time, effort, and money.

My emphasis in this book is on making toys rather than buying them. I encourage people to make toys for several reasons. One is that many of the commercially available toys are expensive, and the amount of attention the toys get from a child doesn't always warrant the expense. Toys made from things found around the house are far more versatile. They can be taken apart, personalized, thrown away when their usefulness is outlived, or modified to suit a child's changing interests and abilities.

Another reason for making toys is that it can provide adults with a form of creative expression and a sense of satisfaction. It's thrilling to watch a child learn from and enjoy something you've created. You're providing experiences and materials to explore that encourage the child's learning and growth.

Making toys also lets you set good examples for children. You're showing them that anything can have play value, even if it isn't made of brightly colored plastic. Seeing the play value in the things around them teaches children to avoid boredom by being resourceful, creative, and inventive. You're also demonstrating how to recycle. Many of the materials used to make the toys in this book would normally become trash.

An added advantage to making your own toys is that you can gear them to your child's level of development, interests, present abilities, and temperament. Throughout the book I encourage you to present new toys and activities in small steps, first introducing the basics and then building on them. In that way, you give your child the opportunity to practice the skills he or she now has a readiness for and then to advance by increments. The reason for this step-by-step approach is that children build self-confidence by experiencing small successes. Being successful also increases children's desire to do more and helps make the challenges they encounter exciting.

Finally, I want to encourage parents to use the information presented here as a starting point. Don't be limited by my ideas. See what your creativity and your child's can produce. And remember that the main purpose of these toys and play activities is for both of you to have fun!

Rita Anderson

iNTRoDUCTioN

It's often said that "play is child's work." Along with being fun, play is a muscle-strengthening and skill-building activity. It aids in developing coordination of the large muscles of the arms, legs, and trunk and the small muscles of the fingers. The toys that children play with are learning tools that can stimulate problem-solving abilities and intellectual growth. Mastering a toy or activity can give children feelings of confidence and competence. These combined benefits of play help ready children for later school and life experiences.

In this book, we offer parents information on the kind of play your child can enjoy as a toddler, how you can enhance the play experience with your child, and the types of toys you can make for your child—toys that are fun to play with, safe, help increase a toddler's concentration and attention span, and challenge a toddler's growing abilities without causing frustration.

Part 1 of this book provides a look at the abilities and interests of toddlers—children one and two years of age. It also includes information on how you can enrich the play experience for your child.

Part 2 describes materials, tools, and supplies to have on hand for making toys. In addition, it offers tips to help you construct toys that are appealing, durable, and safe.

Part 3 contains the information you need to construct over 40 different toys. The toys are grouped into 10 categories, according to their main characteristics or the primary skills they require. Along with instructions for making each toy, you'll find the following:

o Suggestions for ways that you and your child can play with the toy

o Information on the benefits you can help your child derive from these play activities—benefits in the areas of muscle control and coordination, language development, reasoning and problem-solving abilities, and sensory awareness

o Suggestions for questions to ask and things to talk about with your child as you play with the toy

Part 1

Your Toddler and You

○   ❏   △   ◇

One- to Two-Year-Olds

Overview

This chapter contains information on your child's development between one and two years of age. It's provided to help you understand where your child is headed so that you can offer your child appropriate materials and experiences.

Toddler Milestones

This chart lists milestones in the development of one- to two-year-old children. Please keep in mind that the ages and corresponding skills are only approximations. All children have their own developmental timetables.

At this age:	Many toddlers:
12 months	*Sit and stand alone*
	Cruise (hold on and walk)

At this age:	Many toddlers:
	Stoop
	Respond to their name
	Roll a ball
	Say one or two words
	Experience strong anxiety over separation from parent(s)
	Show stranger anxiety
	Eat finger foods
	Show preferences for people, food, and objects
	Remember things
	Associate objects and actions with events (such as associating the high chair with food, or hands extended with the word "up")
13 months	*Understand words*
	Solve simple problems
	Deliberately perform an action to get a result
	Walk
	Use a spoon and cup
	Enjoy looking out the window
	Imitate adult actions
	Show a sense of humor and affection
14 months	*Walk either with or without help*
	Identify sounds and what makes them
	Begin to expand their vocabulary
	Find hidden toys
	Remember where they found an object before
	Untie shoes

At this age:	Many toddlers:
15 months	*Walk alone*
	Climb stairs
	Throw objects
	Stack two to three objects
	Respond to key words
	Say "no"
	Open containers
	Make deliberate crayon marks
	Tear paper
	Enjoy messy play (such as sand, water, and mud play)
16 months	*Squat to pick up objects*
	Walk carrying objects
	Walk sideways
	Participate in rough-house play
	Test adults
	Imitate adult routines (such as cleaning)
17 months	*Climb up on things*
	Walk backwards
	Tug and drag objects
	Increase their explorations
	Name and point to objects
	Look at picture books alone (but prefer company)
18 months	*Run*
	Show some hand preference
	Slide down a slide

At this age:	Many toddlers:
	Walk up stairs with help
	Blow (bubbles, feathers)
	Climb down stairs
	Go to get what they want without asking
19 months	*Listen and move to music*
	Identify main body parts
	Sort two to three objects or shapes
	Stack three to four blocks
	Show a dislike for waiting
20 months	*Say 15 to 20 words and two-word sentences*
	Remember yesterday
	Want things their own way
	Go to get things when asked
	Have tantrums
21 months	*Ride a scooter (or other small riding toy)*
	Point to designated objects in books
	Turn pages of a book
	Hold pictures right-side up
	Match pictures to real objects
	Use and understand the word "mine"
	Want to do things for themselves
	Kick a ball
	Unwrap an object
22 months	*Fit shapes into a three-piece puzzle*
	Put things away

At this age:	Many toddlers:
	Come when called
	Screw and unscrew lids
	Show an interest in insects
	Match animals and sounds
	Model adult behavior
23 months	*Use three-word sentences*
	Talk to themselves
	Enjoy rhymes
	Sing easy repetitive songs
	Brush their teeth with help (mostly imitation)
	Say "please" and "thank you"
	Wash and dry their hands
	Remove their clothes
	Help with household chores
	Recognize places and landmarks
	Show imagination
	Throw a ball
	Enjoy working with their fingers
24 months	*Show an interest in smells*
	Enjoy carrying satchels (such as a purse)
	Walk up stairs without help
	Turn a door knob
	Stir
	Stack six or more blocks
	Jump down from a low object
	Jump in place
	Listen to short stories

At this age:	Many toddlers:
	Open and close zippers
	Follow simple directions (Get the ball. Touch your nose.)
	Ask questions that require one-word answers (Who's that? What's that?)

Play Activities for Toddlers

The following chart shows the types of play activities toddlers enjoy at the different stages of their development. As with the preceding chart, please keep in mind that these readiness ages are only approximations. All children have their own developmental timetables and aptitudes.

At this age:	Toddlers like to:
12 to 15 months	*Crumple and toss paper*
	Fill containers and dump the contents
	Roll objects down hills and inclines
	Turn light switches on and off
	Play with flashlights
	Poke objects into play dough
	Play and sing action songs and rhymes
12 to 18 months	*Paint with edible finger paints (such as pudding)*
	Play in sand and water
	Push and pull toys (such as trains and cars)
	Scribble with crayons

At this age:	Toddlers like to:
	Look at and talk about books, family pictures, photo albums, and catalogs
	Put objects into holes
	Roll a ball
	Nest objects (stack them one inside the other)
	Put large hand-held objects (such as blocks) into holes
15 to 18 months	*Play hide-and-seek*
	Play with finger puppets
	Find and identify the source of sounds (such as an alarm clock or timer)
	Match plastic bottles and lids
	Dance
	Play musical instruments
	Blow bubbles, candles, feathers, paper, a harmonica, a kazoo
18 to 20 months	*Play with a toy hammer*
	Stack objects on a spindle
	Stack large blocks or boxes
	Put small objects (such as pegs) into holes
18 to 24 months	*Put together three- to six-piece puzzles*
	Play on riding toys and rocking horses
	Play with small wooden blocks
	Throw and kick a ball
	Participate in the kitchen by peeling eggs, mashing potatoes, smelling spices, and adding premeasured ingredients

At this age:	Toddlers like to:
	Sort similar and different objects (such as laundry, silverware, blocks)
	Sort and identify shapes
	Play matching games (such as matching pictures to real objects)
	Enjoy digging (in sand, dirt)
21 to 24 months	*Engage in pretend play with dolls and doll accessories, vehicles, toy housekeeping items, a child-sized kitchen, and child-sized furniture*
	Sort large and small items

Playing With Your Child

Overview

Playing with your child has many benefits and rewards. Above all, it's a way for you to enjoy each other. It's also a way to continually renew child/parent bonding as your child grows and changes. And third, it's a way to help your child develop skills, knowledge, and attitudes. This chapter looks at how you can enrich the time you and your child spend as partners in play.

The Purpose of Play

Children are learning all the time. While playing, they acquire, practice, and master skills. Through their early experiences in manipulating play objects, children learn abstract concepts. As they learn, children gain a sense of order and control over their expanding world.

Children learn more when a parent or other adult becomes their "partner in play." The adult enriches the play experience by providing things to explore, helping children talk and think about what they're doing, helping them form ideas about their experiences, and using words to describe those ideas. This child/adult partnership helps children develop their full individual potential.

Presenting Toys and Activities to Your Child

The success of the toys and activities you introduce to your child depends to a large extent on how you present them. Negative attitudes can develop if you present a toy or activity with no instruction, if you criticize your child's attempts, or if your child is unable to achieve success. In any of these situations, frustration sets in and your child may have no interest in trying the toy or activity again.

To avoid frustration and to make playtime a positive and enjoyable experience, keep in mind the following guidelines:

o Set regular times for your shared play. Most children feel more secure with a routine.

o Make sure both you and your child are in the mood to play.

o Focus on only one or two toys—one that's new and one that your child has enjoyed before.

o Describe *and* demonstrate what to do with a new toy. Be a role model. Toddlers love to imitate.

o Encourage your child to try new toys or activities and then subtly guide the child throughout the activity. If he/she is uninterested, wait and try another time. Never push your child to learn.

o Introduce a new toy or activity in a way that allows your child to experience success on the first attempt. That may require guiding your child's hand or positioning the toy in a certain way. If the toy is beyond your child's present abilities, quietly put it away until the child develops a readiness for it. The results will be your child's positive attitude toward both the toy and the play experience and a desire to do more.

o Praise your child's efforts and ignore mistakes. Compliment the little successes each step of the way.

o Keep your shared playtime a pleasant experience. When your child loses interest in a toy, put it away or end the play session.

o Critically view a toy for any unsafe features. If you have any doubts, remake the toy or remain alert and stay with your child whenever he/she plays with it.

Once you've introduced a toy, your child can then play with it independently—especially if you store the toy where it's easily accessible to the child. It's unnecessary for a parent to play with a child all of the time. However, children always appreciate the presence of a responsive adult who observes, encourages, and offers praise.

When you see that your child has mastered a toy, you might want to actively join in the play again. You can then challenge your child to try playing with the toy in a more advanced way or in a totally new way.

When you think your child has outgrown a toy, put it away for a few months. When you reintroduce the toy, you'll find that your child will play with it differently because the child's abilities and maturity level are now different.

Building Confidence

Playtime offers a good opportunity to observe children to determine what their abilities and interests are and what they're showing a readiness for. With this information, parents can choose or adapt toys and activities to their children's current level of development and can help their children gain the confidence they need to advance.

Keep in mind that every skill is made up of subskills. To master a skill, a child must first master each of the subskills that comprise it. Every time you see your child master a subskill, you can encourage him/her to take the activity one step further by suggesting "Now, can you do it this way?" By using this step-by-step approach, you're expanding the range of your child's abilities and building his/her self-confidence with a series of small successes. Success promotes the desire to do and learn more and gives your child pleasure in learning.

Understanding the Importance of Repetition

Repetition is a very important part of a child's learning process. To master a skill and retain it takes practice over a period of time. Although repetition may seem dull to an adult, children like doing familiar things. They strive to perfect their skills and enjoy repeating what they can do well. With each success, children build confidence and a sense of pride. Remember to acknowledge those feelings. Praise your child for each new accomplishment and for his/her effort.

Stimulating Language Development

You can use all daily activities, especially play, to stimulate your child's language development. By talking to your child as you play, your toddler's vocabulary and understanding of language will grow. By asking questions, you'll stretch your toddler's thinking. Remember to just talk naturally, using short sentences and easy-to-understand descriptions.

Part 2

Getting Started

○   ❏   △   ◇

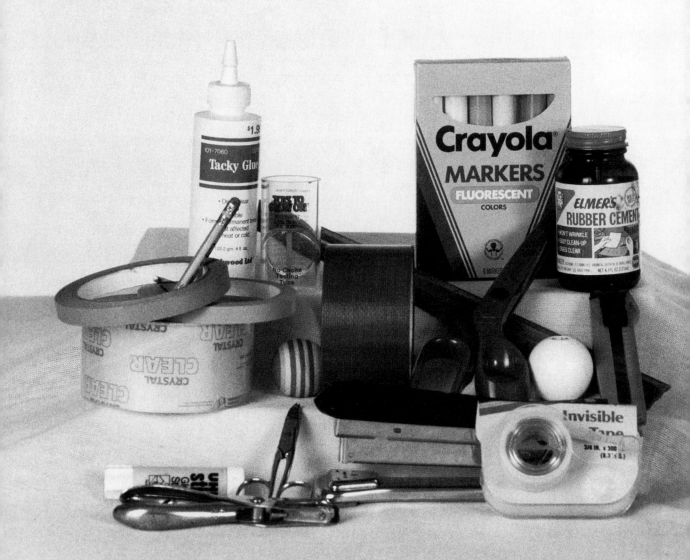

Materials, Tools, and Supplies

Overview

The toys described in this book are simple to make. They require materials found around the house; supplies available at local hardware stores, supermarkets, fabric stores, and craft stores; and some basic tools common to most household tool boxes.

Materials

Many of the items we routinely discard are ideal materials for making toys. Some things to save for toy making are:

○ Paper bags
○ Cardboard boxes—for sturdiness and size, printer's boxes (the kind stationery, computer paper, or copier paper come in) and frozen meat boxes are among the best. Shoe boxes are a convenient size but often need to be reinforced with corrugated cardboard.
○ Cardboard tubes—wide tubes come with products such as paper towels and gift wrap and narrow tubes with items such as fabric softener and plastic wrap. Very durable narrow tubes come on pants hangers from the cleaners.

○ Metal lids—these come in a variety of diameters and thicknesses on products such as frozen juice and baby food.
○ Coffee cans (in small, medium, and large sizes)
○ Waxed cartons from milk and juice
○ Plastic bottles from bleach, vinegar, or water
○ Plastic film canisters from 35mm film
○ Plastic pill bottles
○ Plastic spice bottles with shaker tops
○ Plastic storage containers (from products such as margarine and whipped toppings)
○ Yogurt containers with resealable lids

Tools and Supplies

Toy making is much easier when you have the right tools and supplies for the job. Some useful tools to have on hand are:

○ A utility knife
○ A drill (electric, hand, or push)
○ A yardstick or ruler
○ Scissors (both manicure and household)
○ Brushes for spreading paint and glue
○ A sharp serrated knife—an electric carving knife makes many tasks easier.
○ A stapler

Other tools you might want to use are wire cutters, a hand saw, a hammer, and a glue gun (although some of the glues listed below work just as well).

Supplies to stock up on include:

○ Glue—a wide variety of glues are available. Depending on the toys you're making, you might choose from the following:

- ❏ Shoe Goo for plastics (a product designed to fix rubber-soled athletic shoes)
- ❏ Tacky glue for fabric or other nonsmooth surfaces
- ❏ Glue sticks for paper and pictures
- ❏ Rubber cement for paper and pictures (The advantages that rubber cement has over other types of glue are that it does not bleed through paper or pictures, does not pucker, allows you to easily detach the glued item, and makes it easy to remove excess rubber cement by rubbing.)
- ❏ Contact cement for permanently sealing plastics and other materials
- ❏ Super glue for fastening lids on bottles and jars (This type of glue may not provide the permanent seal that contact cement does.)
- ❏ Spray adhesives (This type of glue is suitable for a variety of uses but tends to be messy.)

○ Tape

- ❏ Craft tape—colorful and available in different widths; appropriate for decoration but lacking in strength and durability
- ❏ Duct tape—a very strong and durable tape that comes in various colors
- ❏ Cellophane packaging tape—a wide tape that's strong, durable, and appropriate for preserving small items (Because of its shiny surface, items covered with this tape look laminated.)
- ❏ Electrical tape—strong but dries out over time
- ❏ Strapping tape—also strong but dries out over time
- ❏ Masking tape—not as strong as some of the other tapes and dries out over time
- ❏ Transparent cellophane tape—a narrow all-purpose tape especially good for fastening paper

○ Paint

- ❏ Latex—nontoxic and easy to clean up
- ❏ Spray—especially good for small items and comes in a variety of colors, including fluorescent and metallic tones

(Tempera and poster paints are also available but have several drawbacks. They get powdery and rub off over time, are more expensive than the other paints listed here, and are not as vibrant.)

○ Cardboard

  ❑ Posterboard—a commonly used and easily available cardboard; available in many types of stores and in an array of colors, including fluorescent
  ❑ Tagboard—a lighter-weight cardboard than posterboard
  ❑ Mat board—a heavy-weight cardboard comparable in thickness to corrugated cardboard
  ❑ Corrugated cardboard—the cardboard used in boxes; varies in sturdiness depending on the corrugation (Printer boxes, frozen meat boxes, and grocery boxes are all a good weight for toy making.)

○ Dowel rods (circular wooden rods available in a variety of widths and lengths)
○ Golf tubes (durable plastic tubes available at sporting goods stores and used to protect golf clubs)
○ Clear adhesive paper (such as Con-Tact brand self-adhesive plastic) for protecting surfaces
○ Miscellaneous items useful in making a variety of toys:

  ❑ Small balls (such as cat toy balls and high fly balls)
  ❑ Wooden clothespins
  ❑ Foam bathtub blocks
  ❑ Round napkin rings
  ❑ Cookie cutters
  ❑ Golf tees
  ❑ Food coloring
  ❑ Metal notebook rings

Tips for Making Toys

Overview

When you're making toys, three important rules to keep in mind are:

○ Make them appealing.
○ Make them durable.
○ Make them safe.

The general guidelines presented in this chapter will help you make toys that both attract a toddler's attention and hold up to a toddler's abuse. The safety considerations will help you construct playthings that present no danger to a young child.

General Guidelines

Research shows that young children prefer primary colors and geometric shapes. By incorporating these in your decorations, you'll create toys that will grab your toddler's attention. A note of caution, however, is don't overdo it. Avoid decorating toys to the point where the decorations are a distraction. For example, if a play activity requires your toddler to find an opening in a box, make sure the opening is clearly visible—that it contrasts with the rest of the box. Otherwise, your child might have difficulty finding the opening and become frustrated with the toy.

As you're constructing a toy, remember that decorations can be functional. For instance, if you need to seal a box with tape, you can choose a colored tape and apply it in a decorative way—by fastening it all the way around the box and lid to make it look like a band.

Also remember to make the toys you build as strong as possible. Otherwise, after heavy use the toy will fall apart, and you'll need to remake it. Some ways to increase a toy's durability are:

○ Use clear adhesive paper (or for small items cellophane packaging tape) to protect surfaces. (If you're covering both sides of an item, extend the adhesive paper or tape beyond the edge of the item to make a clear border around the edge. Then seal it. The result will be a teething-proof, semiwaterproof surface that will be difficult for children to peel back.)
○ Add extra pieces of corrugated cardboard to the inside of boxes and lids to reinforce them.
○ Reinforce the corners and edges of boxes and lids with duct tape.
○ Glue the ends of craft tape to keep children from peeling it off.
○ Reinforce cardboard tubes by stuffing them with newspaper. (Push the newspaper far enough into the tube so that a child can't pull it out. To make the newspaper even less accessible, cover the end of the tube with a circular piece of tape.)

Safety Considerations

Always keep safety in mind as you construct toys. The toys you make (or buy) for a toddler should have:

○ Smooth, rounded edges (with no sharp points or corners)
○ Nontoxic, lead-free paint, which must be thoroughly dried before using the toy
○ Flame-retardant or flame-resistant fabric
○ No glue on the outside (since some glues are toxic and the child may put the object in his/her mouth)
○ Strings or ribbons *less* than 12 inches long (to avoid strangulation)
○ No easily detachable parts
○ No parts made of brittle plastic

○ No potential danger if played with in a different way than intended
○ No parts small enough for a child to swallow, such as beads, marbles, buttons, coins, etc.

It's best to test all small items in the No Choke Testing Tube—Small Objects Tester. Those that fit inside the tube are small enough for a child to choke on and should not be used for toys or games or left within the child's reach. Two sources that carry the No Choke Testing Tube are:

Toys to Grow On
P. O. Box 17
Long Beach, CA 90801

Perfectly Safe Catalog
7245 Whipple Ave. N.W.
N. Canton, OH 44720

Also consider safety when storing toys. Do not store toys in plastic bags. If your child's not yet ready for a toy (for example, if your child puts a foam toy in his/her mouth and bites off pieces), put the toy in an unreachable place and introduce it again later when your child is older. If an older sibling's toys have small pieces, batteries, or surfaces that can be chewed off, store them out of your toddler's reach.

Be sure that toy chests have spring-supported lids. Toy chests without lid supports can injure children or cause suffocation. Spring supports are available from these sources:

Carlson Capital Manufacturing Co.
P. O. Box 6165
Rockford, IL 61125

Perfectly Safe Catalog
7245 Whipple Ave. N.W.
N. Canton, OH 44720

Counter Balance Support Co.
4788 Colt Road
Rockford, IL 61125

In addition, check to see that toy chests have holes or spaces for ventilation.

Part 3

Toys and Activities

Pounding Toys

Overview

The toys in this category include a hammer, either bought or homemade, and something to hit: golf tees, beads, balls, or other objects. Most children are ready for pounding toys between 18 and 20 months of age.

Plastic or wooden hammers are easy to find in toy stores. They're sold alone or as part of other toys. You can also use a wooden meat mallet with the handle shortened to the desired length. An alternative to buying a hammer is to make your own following the instructions given in this chapter.

Purpose

Important benefits of pounding toys are that they provide an outlet for aggressive feelings and a channel for a child's high level of energy. In addition, pounding activities help develop the following in children:

- Upper-arm and grip strength
- Eye-hand coordination

○ Finger dexterity and two-hand coordination (when fitting a golf tee, clothespin, or other object into a hole and holding it steady for pounding)

Toys You Can Make:

○ Hammer
○ Pound the Seesaw
○ Clothespin Hammering
○ Golf Tee Hammering
○ Pound the Balls
○ Pound and Roll

The instructions for making these toys follow.

Hammer

WHAT YOU'LL NEED

- Two dowel rods, ½ inch in diameter and 1¼ inches in diameter
- A hand saw
- Sandpaper
- A drill (manual or electric)
- Wood glue
- A small screw (optional)
- Nontoxic lead-free latex or spray paint (optional)

STEPS TO FOLLOW

1. Cut the ½-inch dowel rod to a length of 6 inches to make the handle of the hammer.
2. Cut the 1¼-inch dowel rod to a length of about 2 inches. This piece will be the head of the hammer.
3. Sand any rough edges.
4. Drill a ½-inch hole ¾ inch deep in the middle of the hammer head and fill it with wood glue.
5. Insert the handle into the hole.
6. For added strength, insert a small screw in the top of the hammer head to connect it securely to the handle.
7. If you like, paint the hammer with nontoxic paint.

Pound the Seesaw

WHAT YOU'LL NEED

○ A cylinder, which can be any of the following:

- ❏ Several sheets of newspaper rolled up tightly and rubber banded
- ❏ A magazine rolled up tightly and rubber banded
- ❏ A sturdy cardboard tube reinforced by stuffing it with newspaper (The tubes that come with dryer fabric softener sheets or plastic wrap—about 1 inch in diameter—work well. Paper towel tubes are too large unless you're using a book bigger than 8½ × 11 inches.)

○ An 8½ × 11 inch hardcover book
○ A small lightweight object, such as a stuffed toy, bean bag, or rolled sock
○ A small hammer (either purchased or homemade)

ACTIVITY

Place the cylinder on a flat surface, either the table or floor. Center the book on top of the cylinder with one end down and the other end in the air. Put the small lightweight object on the low end of the book and have your child hit the high end of the book with the hammer. The small object will fly into the air.

VARIATION

Place a stuffed animal on each side of the book and pretend that it's a seesaw ride at the park.

THINGS TO TALK ABOUT

Some things to discuss as your child pounds the seesaw, are:

○ Where the object landed: "Did it land in the same place as last time?"
○ How high it went: "Did you hit it higher than the windowsill? Higher than your head?"
○ How hard it was hit: "Did you give it a tap or a pound?"
○ Cause and effect: "What happens each time you hit the book?"

Clothespin Hammering

WHAT YOU'LL NEED

- A cardboard egg carton
- Scissors or utility knife
- Wooden clothespins with rounded ends
- Nontoxic lead-free spray paint (optional)
- A small hammer (either purchased or homemade)

STEPS TO FOLLOW

1. Turn the cardboard egg carton upside down and cut small holes in the bottom of each egg compartment. The holes should be the diameter of the rounded end of the clothespins.
2. If you choose, decorate the carton and clothespins with spray paint.

ACTIVITY

Hold the clothespins or poke them into the upside-down egg carton just far enough to make them stand upright. Then let the child use a hammer to pound the clothespins into the holes. Children who aren't yet ready for pounding can just push them down into the holes.

VARIATIONS

○ Instead of clothespins, use sections of the cardboard tube that comes on pants hangers from the cleaners.

○ In place of the egg carton, use a thin cardboard box with a lid. For instructions on how to make this toy, see *Clothespin Pegboard* in the chapter *Pegboard Toys*.

THINGS TO TALK ABOUT

Some things to discuss with this activity are:

○ Colors (if the clothespins are decorated): "You sure did a good job of hammering in all of those red clothespins!"

○ Numbers: "How many times did you hit that clothespin?" "How many holes are there?" "Is there one clothespin for each hole?"

○ Degree: "How did you hit that clothespin—hard or soft?"

○ Directions: "You put a clothespin in the top hole."

Golf Tee Hammering

WHAT YOU'LL NEED

- Golf tees
- A box—corrugated cardboard box, gift box, etc.
- Nontoxic lead-free latex or spray paint, colored or patterned adhesive paper, or craft tape to decorate the box (optional)
- A small hammer (either purchased or homemade)

> *Safety note:* Children who put things in their mouths require close supervision when playing with golf tees. Sandpaper or an emery board may be used to dull the pointed ends on the golf tees. Children who are still teething or who put objects in their mouths should use only giant golf tees. Some sporting goods stores sell giant 2-inch golf tees that won't fit completely inside the no-choke test tube.

ACTIVITY

Hold the golf tee upright or poke it into the box just far enough to make the tee stand up. Then let the child pound the golf tee into the surface of the box. Later, children might enjoy using the box as a pegboard, reinserting golf tees in existing holes. For additional suggestions, see the chapter *Pegboard Toys*.

THINGS TO TALK ABOUT

Some things to discuss with this activity are:

○ Colors: "You pounded in all of the blue 'nails.'"
○ Numbers: "You hit the 'nail' three times." "You made five holes." "Let's count how many 'nails' you pounded into the box."
○ Directions and spatial concepts: "You pounded a white 'nail' at the top of the box (or next to a red one, between the blue ones, etc.)."

Pound
the Balls

WHAT YOU'LL NEED

- A heavy box—a mailing box or frozen meat box (usually white and corrugated). If a heavy box is not available, use a shoe box and reinforce the lid by taping corrugated cardboard inside.
- A utility knife or scissors
- Two ½ inch-wide strips of elastic cut about as long as the top of the box
- A stapler
- Nontoxic, lead-free latex or spray paint, colored or patterned adhesive paper, or craft tape (optional)
- Small balls (High fly balls, plastic practice golf balls, or sturdy cat toy balls are good choices for this activity. You can also use large wooden beads or spools.)
- A small hammer (either purchased or homemade)

> **Safety note:** Avoid using Ping-Pong balls, which develop sharp points when dented. Golf balls may be used but can be dangerous when thrown. Test any balls or beads used in the No Choke Testing Tube—Small Objects Tester to be sure they are too large to swallow. For additional information on this product, see the section on safety considerations in the chapter *Tips for Making Toys*.

STEPS TO FOLLOW

1. Cut three holes in the lid of the box. Make them evenly spaced and large enough for the balls (or other objects) to fit through.
2. On the inside of the lid, staple two pieces of elastic—one covering the top of the holes and one covering the bottom. Leave a narrow slit along the middle of the holes uncovered. The elastic strips will provide resistance as your child pounds the objects into the holes.
3. Put the lid on the box. If you choose, decorate the box with paint, adhesive paper, or craft tape.

ACTIVITY

Place the balls (or other objects) on top of the holes and let your child hammer (or push) them in. Then lift the lid, remove the balls, and start the game again.

VARIATIONS

○ Make this a color-matching activity by drawing circles around each hole in colors that match the balls or other pounding objects.
○ Make it a size-matching activity by having pounding objects and holes of different sizes.

○ Make it a shape-matching activity by using different wooden shapes, such as a square, tri-angle, and circle, in place of balls, beads, or spools. (For information on making the wooden shapes, see the shape-sorting activities in the chapter *Stacking, Sorting, and Nesting Toys*.)

○ To use the toy without a hammer, have your child push the objects through the holes.

THINGS TO TALK ABOUT

Some things to discuss with this activity are:

○ The number of times your child hits the object
○ How hard your child has to hit or push the object to make it go into the hole
○ The color, size, or shape of each object your child hits
○ Whether another object, such as a spool, will fit into the same hole where your child hit the ball

Pound
and Roll

WHAT YOU'LL NEED

○ All supplies needed for the previous toy, *Pound the Balls;* plus:
○ A cardboard tube (from paper towels, aluminum foil, waxed paper, etc.) or a plastic golf
   tube (See the description in *Materials, Tools, and Supplies* in Part 2.)
○ A piece of corrugated cardboard
○ Glue
○ Tape, such as duct tape
○ A small hammer (either purchased or homemade)

STEPS TO FOLLOW

1. Follow steps 1 and 2 for making the previous toy, *Pound the Balls.*
2. Make a ball slide to place inside the box by following these steps:

   a. Cut a cardboard or plastic golf tube in half lengthwise.
   b. Trim the tube to a length about ¼ inch longer than the diagonal length of the box. The
      tube must reach from the upper corner of one narrow side of the box down to the lower
      corner of the opposite narrow side and out a hole that you'll cut in the lower corner.

3. Make a support for the ball slide out of corrugated cardboard:

   a. Cut a piece of corrugated cardboard to fit in one of the narrow ends of the box. This cardboard support will go under the high end of the ball slide. The support must be low enough to allow the ball to drop down from the hole and onto the ball slide without getting stuck.

   b. Cut a U-shaped notch in the top of the support, wide enough to insert the ball slide.

   c. Glue the support to the inside of the box.

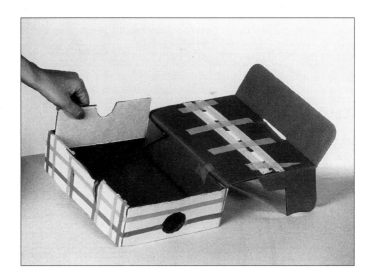

4. On the other narrow side of the box, cut a hole in the lower corner where the ball will roll out. To make certain the exit hole is the right size, trace the ball on the side of the box; then cut the hole slightly larger than the circle you traced.

5. Rest one end of the ball slide on its support, making sure that the other end extends out of the hole in the lower corner of the box. The ball slide should be positioned so that it will be directly under the holes cut in the top of the box.

6. Put the lid on the box and test the ball slide to make sure that the balls can roll freely from the top of the slide down to the bottom and out the exit hole. If balls get stuck, you may need to shorten the cardboard support or enlarge the exit hole.

7. Tape or glue the ball slide in place.

8. Reinforce the portion of the tube that extends out of the box by applying tape to the underside where the tube and box meet. Duct tape works well and can be applied in a decorative way.

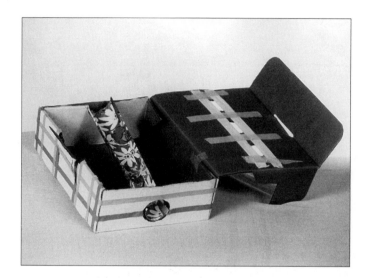

ACTIVITY

Have your child hammer or push the balls into the holes, just as with the previous toy, *Pound the Balls*. But instead of lifting the lid to remove the balls, the balls will roll down the slide and out the hole in the side of the box. When your child is finished playing with the toy, you can store the hammer and balls inside the box.

VARIATIONS

See the preceding toy description, *Pound the Balls*.

THINGS TO TALK ABOUT

See the preceding toy description, *Pound the Balls*.

Incline Toys

Overview

Incline toys demonstrate to children the effects of gravity. In playing with these toys, children roll objects down tubes or troughs and watch for the objects to reach the bottom. The objects they roll might be balls, large beads, toy cars and trucks, or even homemade objects such as a wad of paper or tape. This type of play begins to appeal to children at approximately 12 to 15 months of age.

Purpose

Overall, playing with incline toys helps children increase their concentration and attention span because the results can vary each time they play with the toy. For example, children can roll different types of objects down the incline, or they can increase or decrease the incline. The individual activities involved in this type of play help develop the following in children:

○ Finger dexterity and eye-hand coordination (placing a ball or other round object in a tube or trough)
○ An understanding of gravity and of cause and effect (seeing that releasing a ball on an incline causes the ball to roll down)

○ Anticipation (wondering where the ball will come out and, in time, predicting outcomes—how fast the ball will go, when it will roll out of the tube, and which way it will go)
○ Visual tracking (watching the ball roll down an open trough)
○ Directionality (watching the ball roll from top to bottom, from back to front, and from side to side)
○ Spatial awareness (watching the ball roll into a box and out again)

Toys You Can Make:

○ Simple Ball Slide
○ Double Ball Slide
○ Triple Ball Slide

The instructions for making these toys follow.

Simple
Ball Slide

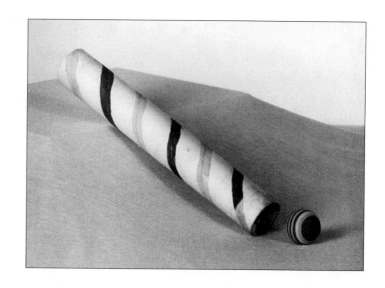

WHAT YOU'LL NEED

○ Objects that roll easily through the tube. Among the objects you can use are:

- ❑ Cat toy balls
- ❑ Large wooden beads
- ❑ High fly balls
- ❑ Plastic practice golf balls
- ❑ Small toy cars or trucks
- ❑ Paper or tape wadded up into a ball

○ A tube (cardboard or plastic golf tube)

Safety note: Avoid using Ping-Pong balls, which develop sharp points when dented. Golf balls may be used, but can be dangerous when thrown. Test any balls or beads used in the No Choke Testing Tube—Small Objects Tester to be sure they are too large to swallow. For additional information on this product, see the section on safety considerations in the chapter *Tips for Making Toys*. Check toy cars and trucks to be sure all pieces (e.g., wheels) are securely attached.

ACTIVITY

Show your toddler how to place a ball (or other object) in the tube and how to angle the tube so that the ball rolls out. Encourage your child to experiment with different angles to make the ball roll faster, slower, or farther. If your child is interested, keep track of the distance the ball rolls each time by marking its stopping point.

VARIATIONS

○ Instead of having your child hold the tube, prop it up on whatever is available, such as books, blocks, a pillow, etc. Try propping up the tube on several different objects and see how far the ball rolls each time.
○ Cut the tube in half lengthwise to make a trough. Your toddler can then watch the ball as it rolls.
○ Set up two tubes or troughs and see which one causes the ball to roll faster or farther.

THINGS TO TALK ABOUT

Some questions to ask about the simple ball slide are:

○ "How did you hold the tube? Did you tilt it or hold it straight up and down?"
○ "Did the ball take longer to come out when you tilted the tube?"
○ "Did the ball roll to the same place as before?"
○ "Did the ball roll farther this time than before?"
○ "Did the ball roll farther than the car?"
○ "Did the bead roll faster than the paper ball?"

Double Ball Slide

Neil Schierstedt

WHAT YOU'LL NEED

- A shoe box or reinforced cardboard box, such as a frozen meat box
- A utility knife or manicure scissors (Manicure scissors work well for cutting circular holes since the scissor blades are curved.)
- Two cardboard or plastic tubes (A plastic golf tube cut to the lengths you wish works best because of its durability.)
- Colored duct tape
- Varnish (optional)
- Paint, colored or patterned adhesive paper, or craft tape (optional)
- Objects that roll (For a list, see *Simple Ball Slide*, earlier in this chapter.)

STEPS TO FOLLOW

1. On one of the wide sides of the box, cut a hole in the lower-left portion. (We'll refer to this side as the front of the box.) The hole should be slightly larger than the diameter of the tube. Also make sure to leave enough space between the hole and the play surface for the ball to exit.
2. On the back of the box, cut another hole in the upper-left portion. Again, make the hole slightly larger than the diameter of the tube.

3. Insert a tube through these holes so that it extends about ¼ inch beyond the bottom hole.

4. Reinforce the portion of the tube that extends beyond the bottom hole with duct tape. Apply the tape to the underside of the tube and to the surrounding area on the box.

5. Follow steps 1 through 4 to cut another pair of holes on the right side of the box. Then insert the second tube and reinforce it with tape. The tubes should be parallel.

6. To give the tubes added durability, dip the ends in varnish and let them harden.

7. If you choose, decorate the box and the tubes with paint, colored or patterned adhesive paper, or craft tape. Making each tube a different color or pattern helps children keep track of where they inserted the ball (or other object) and where it will exit. For example, children see that if they put the ball in the red tube at the top, it comes out the red tube at the bottom.

ACTIVITY

With each tube, have your toddler insert the rolling object at the top and watch to see what happens. Encourage your child to predict which of the two holes the object will roll out of. If your child is interested, keep track of the distance each object rolls by marking its stopping point with a piece of masking tape or a toy.

VARIATION

Match rolling objects and tubes by color and size. For example, roll the red ball down the red tube; or roll the big ball down the big tube and the small ball down the small tube.

THINGS TO TALK ABOUT

Some questions to ask about the double ball slide are:

o "Where will the ball come out if we put it in this tube?"
o "Where do you think the ball will roll?"
o "If we put balls in each tube right now, will they come out at the same time?"
o "Did the red ball go farther than the blue bead?"
o "Did the ball from the red tube go farther than the ball from the blue tube?"
o "Which bead rolled out the fastest?"

Triple Ball Slide

Neil Schierstedt

WHAT YOU'LL NEED

- A reinforced rectangular cardboard box (approximately 8½ × 11 inches) that is stable when stood up on its side (Gift boxes are unstable because of the ridge the removable lid makes.)
- Three cardboard or plastic tubes (Plastic golf tubes are durable.)
- A utility knife or manicure scissors (Manicure scissors work well for cutting circular holes since the scissor blades are curved.)
- Colored duct tape
- Varnish (optional)
- Paint, colored or patterned adhesive paper, or craft tape
- Objects that roll (For a list, see *Simple Ball Slide*, earlier in this chapter.)

STEPS TO FOLLOW

1. Follow steps 1 through 5 for making the previous toy, double ball slide, with one exception. Place the two sets of holes anywhere on the box. (You needn't place them side by side as with the double ball slide.)
2. Cut a third pair of angled holes in opposite sides of the box and insert a tube through these holes. The third tube will cross the other two inside the box.
3. Again, use colored duct tape to reinforce the tube where it extends beyond the box.

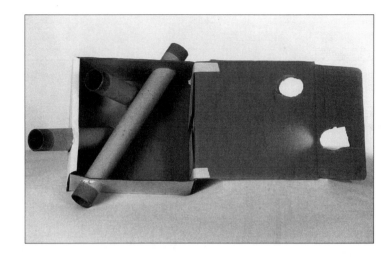

4. If you would like to make the ends of the tubes more durable, dip them in varnish and let them harden.

5. If you choose, decorate the box and the tubes with paint, colored or patterned adhesive paper, or craft tape. Making each tube a different color or pattern helps children keep track of where they inserted the ball (or other object) and where it will exit. For example, children see that if they put the ball in the red tube at the top, it comes out the red tube at the bottom.

ACTIVITY

See the preceding toy description, *Double Ball Slide.*

VARIATION

See the preceding toy description, *Double Ball Slide.*

THINGS TO TALK ABOUT

See the preceding toy description, *Double Ball Slide.*

Blocks

Overview

Children usually begin to enjoy playing with blocks at around 18 months. They often start by stacking large blocks or boxes and then, by 24 months, enjoy building with smaller blocks.

Blocks come in a wide range of sizes, colors, shapes, textures, and types, from ABC blocks to building blocks. You can buy blocks made from such materials as wood, cardboard, fabric, foam, or plastic. Some plastic blocks are also magnetic, one of the easiest kinds of blocks for toddlers to build with. In addition to buying blocks, you can make your own. This chapter describes how.

Activities

The ways in which children can play with blocks are limited only by their imagination. Among the activities children enjoy are:

○ Playing hide-and-seek—searching for a small toy that has been hidden inside of a block structure
○ Filling a container with blocks and dumping them out

○ Lining up blocks in a row (to make a wall, a fence, a train that moves by pushing the last block, etc.)

○ Stacking blocks to build structures

○ Balancing blocks (especially challenging when trying to balance blocks of different sizes and shapes)

○ Sorting blocks by characteristics, such as color, texture (when using fabric-covered blocks), or shape (cubes, cylinders, etc.)

○ Knocking down blocks by:

❑ Using parts of their bodies: hands, feet, head (appropriate with soft blocks), or the whole body (walking into the block structure)

❑ Pushing a toy, such as a car or a truck, into the blocks

❑ Rolling a ball (For toddlers, the best way to roll a ball is sitting on the floor with their legs spread apart and the ball placed between their legs. They then push the ball with both hands. If toddlers use only one hand, they tend to push the ball off to the side instead of straight ahead.)

○ Using blocks in water play—taking sponge blocks or other types of floating blocks in the bathtub or swimming pool (Children might try to stack blocks in the water or balance a toy on top of a block.) Watch children so they do not bite off pieces of the blocks

○ Engaging in imaginative play—pretending that lined up blocks are a wall or a train; that stacked blocks are buildings or cities; that floating blocks are boats

○ Using sponge or wooden blocks with paint or ink to do printing (See the chapter *Messy Play Activities* for additional information.)

Purpose

Engaging in these various types of block play helps children develop the following:

○ Muscle control and coordination (especially whole-body control when children are building structures with large blocks and eye-hand coordination when they are positioning blocks)

○ Anticipation. Children observe and learn to predict what will happen when they place one block on top of another or when they roll a ball or toy car into a stack of blocks.

○ An understanding of cause and effect. Children see that when they perform an action—walking into a tower of blocks—something happens: blocks go crashing to the ground.

○ Visual discrimination (how objects are the same and different)

○ Perception of size (small, big)

○ Perception of shape (circle, square, triangle)

○ Sense of balance (when building a structure with blocks)

○ Directionality (The red block is at the top of the stack; the blue one is at the bottom.)

○ Spatial awareness (One block is next to another. The square block is beneath the cylindrical block.)

In addition to these benefits, playing with cloth-covered blocks provides children with sensory stimulation.

Things to Talk About

Some things to discuss as your child plays with blocks are:

○ Shapes: "I'm stacking the square blocks to make a big building."

○ Sizes: "Here's a short stack of blocks; here's a tall stack."

○ Directions: "We're lining up the blocks side by side." "Our block tower is going up, up, up."

○ Colors and patterns: "Let's stack the red blocks." "Where's the blue-striped block?" "Can you find the block with the picture of a cat?"

○ Textures: "Does this block feel smooth or rough?" "Which blocks are soft and fuzzy?" "Are the fuzzy blocks hard to stack?"

○ Spatial concepts: "The blue block is under the red one."

○ Numbers: "Let's count the number of blocks in this stack." "We put four blocks in a row to make this fence."

○ Sounds: "The blocks went 'crash' when you knocked them down." "What sound does the block in your hand make when you shake it?"

○ Comparisons: "This tower is higher than that one."

Toys You Can Make:

○ Crazy Blocks
○ Cardboard Blocks
○ Carton Blocks
○ Round Blocks
○ Foam Blocks
○ Floating Blocks
○ Wooden Building Blocks

The instructions for making these toys follow.

Crazy Blocks

WHAT YOU'LL NEED

- Paper bags in small and/or large sizes, such as lunch bags and grocery bags
- Newspaper
- Tape
- Spray paint (optional)

STEPS TO FOLLOW

1. Stuff each bag with newspaper.
2. Fold over the top of each bag and tape it shut.
3. If you choose, decorate the bags with spray paint. Try using a variety of colors and patterns, such as stripes and dots. (This is a good way to use up left-over spray paint.)

ACTIVITY

Crazy blocks are soft and don't balance well. That makes them appropriate for fun but not for building. Children enjoy tossing crazy blocks, making stacks of them topple, and crashing into them with their bodies or objects. Crazy blocks are lightweight and appropriate for this type of play.

THINGS TO TALK ABOUT

See the beginning of this chapter.

Cardboard Blocks

WHAT YOU'LL NEED

- Gift boxes in a variety of shapes and sizes
- Newspaper (optional)
- Tape
- Nontoxic lead-free latex or spray paint, colored or patterned adhesive paper, colored craft tape, or plastic tape for decorating (optional)

STEPS TO FOLLOW

1. If you want to make the boxes more durable, stuff them with newspaper.
2. Tape the lids of the boxes shut.
3. If you choose, decorate the boxes in one of the following ways:

   a. Cover them with adhesive paper in a variety of colors or patterns.
   b. Apply strips of colored tape to them.
   c. Paint designs on them, such as dots or stripes. (This is a good way to use up leftover paint.)

ACTIVITY

These boxes are good for stacking and toppling. Because the boxes are lightweight, children can crash into them with their heads or entire bodies without getting hurt. Children also enjoy lining up the boxes and pushing them like a train.

VARIATION

For more uniformly-sized blocks, use tissue boxes instead of gift boxes. Stuff them with newspaper and cover the open side with a piece of cardboard. Then decorate the boxes by covering them with colored or patterned adhesive paper.

THINGS TO TALK ABOUT

See the beginning of this chapter.

Carton Blocks

WHAT YOU'LL NEED

- Waxed cartons from milk or juice in either the ½-gallon size for large blocks or the 10-ounce size for small blocks (A good source for small cartons is school cafeterias.)
- Utility knife or scissors
- Nontoxic lead-free latex paint, textured fabric and tacky glue, or colored or patterned adhesive paper for decorating (optional)

STEPS TO FOLLOW

For each block:

1. Rinse out two cartons of the same size and cut off the tops with a utility knife or scissors.
2. Slide the cut end of one carton completely into the cut end of the other to form the block.
3. If you choose, decorate the cartons in one of the following ways:

   a. Paint them with latex paint. (Even though the surface is waxed, latex paint will adhere to it.)

b. Glue textured fabric to the blocks. (Tacky glue, available at craft stores, adheres well to fabric.)

c. Cover the blocks with adhesive paper, using a variety of colors or patterns.

ACTIVITY

Due to their uniform size, blocks made from cartons line up and stack well. Because they're lightweight, these blocks are appropriate for crashing into and for toppling. The wax coating on carton blocks makes them more durable than cardboard blocks (either homemade or purchased).

THINGS TO TALK ABOUT

See the beginning of this chapter.

Round Blocks

WHAT YOU'LL NEED

○ Any of the following:

- ❏ Frozen juice containers with peel-off lids
- ❏ Round cardboard containers from oatmeal or cornmeal
- ❏ Round plastic storage containers with lids
- ❏ Plastic pill or vitamin bottles
- ❏ Coffee cans with lids

> **Safety note:** Pound down the inside rim of the coffee cans to avoid sharp edges.

- ❏ Super glue

○ Colored or patterned adhesive paper or craft tape for decorating the containers (optional)

STEPS TO FOLLOW

1. Thoroughly clean out the containers and let dry.
2. Attach the lids with super glue.
3. If you choose, decorate the round blocks with colored or patterned adhesive paper or with craft tape.

ACTIVITY

These blocks give children the opportunity to work with round shapes. In addition to stacking the blocks, children can roll them. If you use a variety of containers, you can also have your child find those that look alike.

VARIATION

Place objects that make different sounds inside the containers. For safety, either use objects that cannot fit into the No Choke Testing Tube—Small Objects Tester (described in Part 2, *Tips for Making Toys*) or use small digestible food items, such as cake sprinkles. Discuss with your child the different sounds inside the blocks and the combination of sounds when the blocks all fall. Ask your toddler to find two blocks that sound alike.

THINGS TO TALK ABOUT

See the beginning of this chapter.

Foam Blocks

WHAT YOU'LL NEED

○ Electric carving knife or other sharp knife
○ Upholstery foam at least 2 inches thick (sold in upholstery and fabric stores in large pieces)
○ Fabric to cover the blocks (optional)

> **Safety note:** Foam blocks should be covered with fabric for children who are still teething or who put objects in their mouths. Otherwise, children may bite off pieces of foam.

STEPS TO FOLLOW

1. Using the carving knife, cut the foam into a variety of shapes and sizes.
2. If you choose, cover the blocks with fabric. Try using multiple colors, patterns, and textures to provide children with sensory stimulation. Two ways to cover blocks are:

   a. Make each surface of the block a different color or texture.
   b. Cover a whole block with the same fabric by wrapping it in the same way you wrap a present, securing the ends of the fabric by stitching or gluing them in place.

ACTIVITY

Children can easily line up foam blocks and stack them. Because they're lightweight, the blocks are appropriate for crashing into and for toppling; and they're one of the few types of blocks your child can safely throw. If you cover the blocks with fabric, you can also have your toddler match two blocks of the same texture, color, or pattern.

THINGS TO TALK ABOUT

If your child is playing with fabric-covered blocks, you can discuss their textures and colors. For additional ideas, see the beginning of this chapter.

Floating Blocks

WHAT YOU'LL NEED

○ Electric carving knife or other sharp knife
○ Sponges or purchased bathtub blocks (These blocks are made of a dense foam material that floats and are usually pastel-colored. They stick to smooth surfaces and to each other when wet.)

STEPS TO FOLLOW

Use the knife to cut the sponges into a variety of shapes and sizes. To make cutting easier, make the sponges stiff by first wetting them and then letting them dry.

ACTIVITY

Floating blocks are lightweight and appropriate for stacking, crashing into, toppling, and throwing. While children can enjoy them outside the water, these blocks offer the widest range of activities and challenges in the bathtub or swimming pool. For example, children can squeeze sponge blocks, stick bathtub blocks to the side of the tub, and can push both types of blocks under the water and watch them pop up again. Children can also throw the blocks and make a splash.

Stacking blocks on a fluid surface is a very different experience for children than stacking them on a solid surface. Also challenging is trying to balance one or more toys on top of a floating block as though the block were a boat.

Safety note: Children who are still teething or who put objects in their mouths will need close supervision when playing with sponge or bathtub blocks because they may bite off pieces of the blocks.

THINGS TO TALK ABOUT

You can discuss all of the topics listed at the beginning of this chapter plus the following:

○ "Can you squeeze the water out of the sponge? Out of the bathtub block?"
○ "Does the big sponge hold a toy better than the little one?"
○ "Can you put enough toys on the sponge to make it sink?"
○ "Can you stack the sponges? What about the bathtub blocks?"
○ "Will the bathtub blocks stick to the side of the tub? Will the sponges?"
○ "What happens when you push the sponge block to the bottom of the tub?"
○ "Did water drip on you when you threw the wet sponge up?"

Wooden Building Blocks

WHAT YOU'LL NEED

- Wood scraps, which may be available from a lumberyard, a carpenter, or a furniture or cabinet maker (You can leave these scraps in the irregular shapes in which they come, cut them yourself into the shapes you choose, or have them cut.)
- Sandpaper
- Paint (optional)

> **Safety note:** Because of chemicals, avoid using scraps cut from pressure-treated lumber.

STEPS TO FOLLOW

1. Sand any rough edges on the wood blocks and slightly round each edge and corner.
2. If you choose, paint the blocks. However, keep in mind that color can be distracting to children. They may not notice that one red and one blue square block put together are the same size as one green rectangular block. Children tend to play more freely with unpainted building blocks.

Activity

Encourage your toddler to create different types of structures with the building blocks—from walls and fences to buildings, bridges, streets, and cities. Also show your child how to run toy cars and trucks through the pretend city streets and how to use the toy vehicles or other toys to knock down the block structures.

You can enhance imaginative play by creating a pretend person with your index and middle fingers to walk around the buildings or through the city streets. To make the pretend person more realistic, draw eyes on your knuckles and a mouth between your fingers.

Things to Talk About

See the beginning of this chapter.

Stacking, Sorting, and Nesting Toys

Overview

The toys in this category are colorful and have great appeal. They engage children in stacking objects and in sorting them by size, shape, and color, all with little guidance from adults. Children begin showing interest in stacking and sorting activities around 18 months of age. They begin by stacking large objects, such as blocks or boxes, on top of one another or by stacking objects, such as rings, on a spindle.

Nesting toys are any containers or objects that fit into one another. To make the pieces nest, children must sort them by size. In most cases, when they turn the nesting pieces upside down, children can stack them, starting with the largest and ending with the smallest.

Children between 12 and 18 months of age enjoy simple nesting activities in which they stack two or three objects inside one another. As they approach two years of age, children are better able to sort big and small items and can manage to nest and stack a larger number of objects.

While toys in this category provide toddlers with much enjoyment, they can also be frustrating. For example, one spindle toy on the market has a rounded base. As children attempt to stack the rings, the spindle can rock back and forth, causing toddlers to miss the spindle.

A classic sorting toy is a bucket with different-shaped openings cut in the lid. Children fit square, round, and triangular (or sometimes rectangular) blocks into the proper openings. Some of the sorting buckets available in stores confuse children. Either they offer too many shapes, or they include two shapes that, to young children, appear to be the same—the square and the rectangle. Both shapes have corners and the same number of sides.

Commercially available nesting toys can frustrate children by not providing enough finger room between the edges for them to manipulate one object inside the other. If children hit their fingers on the upper side or rim, they often give up, assuming that the object won't fit.

One way to eliminate these kinds of frustration for your child is to make your own stacking, sorting, and nesting toys. In this chapter you'll find out how.

Purpose

Stacking, sorting, and nesting tasks are prereading activities. They help to develop the following:

○ Visual discrimination (how objects are the same and different)
○ Perception of size (small, big)
○ Perception of shape (circle, square, triangle, rectangle)
○ Perception of color
○ Perception of volume (The small cups fit inside the large cups.)
○ Directionality (The red cup is at the *top* of the stack; the blue one is at the *bottom*.)
○ Spatial awareness (The ring is *on* the spindle; it's *off* the spindle. One cup is *on top* of another. A block is *inside* the container.)
○ Eye-hand coordination
○ Finger dexterity

Recommendations

Your toddler can more readily gain the benefits that stacking, sorting, and nesting toys offer if you reduce the difficulties these toys can present. Do this by gradually introducing each stacking, sorting, and nesting activity. Let your child experience success with one size, shape, or color before going on to the next.

Things to Talk About

Some things to discuss as your child plays with the toys in this category are:

○ Shapes: "This block is round; this one is square."
○ Sizes: "This opening is long; that one is short." "This container is small; that one is big."
○ Colors: "Let's stack the red rings on the red spindle." "Can you put this blue shape in the blue opening?"
○ Spatial concepts: "You put all of the blocks inside the container." "Will this shape fit through that opening?"
○ Directions: "You put the red cup at the top of the stack; the blue cup is at the bottom."
○ Numbers: "Let's count the number of rings we're stacking." "We dropped three blocks into the container."
○ Volume: "The container is empty; the container is full." "This cup fits inside the other one."

Toys You Can Make:

○ Linking Ring Stacker
○ Napkin Ring Stacker
○ Shape Sorter Toy
○ Size Sorter Toy
○ Sorting Hook Board
○ Mail Box Sorter
○ Nesting Containers
○ Nesting Shapes

The instructions for making these toys follow.

Linking Ring Stacker

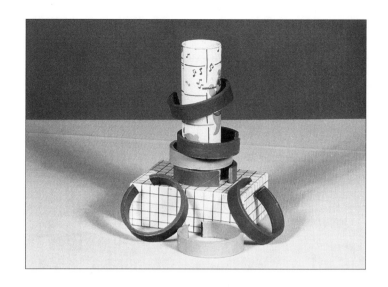

WHAT YOU'LL NEED

- A utility knife
- A small box (such as a child's shoe box or frozen meat box)
- A narrow cardboard tube (paper towel, gift wrap, or other)
- Nontoxic lead-free latex or spray paint
- Colored or patterned adhesive paper or craft tape (optional)
- Newspaper
- Glue (such as contact cement)
- A hand saw
- A wide cardboard mailing tube

STEPS TO FOLLOW

1. Using a utility knife, cut a hole in the center of the box lid. Make it the diameter of the narrow cardboard tube.
2. If you like, decorate the box using latex or spray paint, colored or patterned adhesive paper, or craft tape.
3. Stuff the narrow cardboard tube with wadded-up newspaper to strengthen it. Be sure to

push the newspaper far enough inside the tube so that your child won't be tempted to pull it out. If you choose, decorate the tube with paint, colored or patterned adhesive paper, or craft tape.

4. Insert the narrow cardboard tube in the hole, anchoring it to the bottom of the box with glue.

5. Using a hand saw, slice the wide cardboard mailing tube into 1-inch rings.

6. Cut a notch about $1/2$ inch wide out of each ring. (That way, children can use the rings for linking as well as stacking.)

7. Paint the rings with different colors of latex or spray paint. (Primary colors—red, yellow, blue—are especially appealing to children.)

ACTIVITY

Show your toddler how to stack the rings on the spindle. Begin by having your child hold the ring while you aim the spindle through it. Later, place the spindle on the floor, between your child's legs, and help him/her put the rings on it.

VARIATION

In addition to stacking the rings, children can link them together to make a chain or hook them over something, such as a narrow arm or back of a kitchen chair, a clothes hanger (either plastic or padded), a clothesline, or the edge of a box. You may find, however, that this activity is too difficult for very young toddlers.

THINGS TO TALK ABOUT

See the beginning of this chapter.

Napkin Ring Stacker

WHAT YOU'LL NEED

- A utility knife
- A small box (such as a shoe box or frozen meat box)
- Three small cardboard tubes (such as those that come with clear kitchen plastic wrap)
- Napkin rings in three different colors (Primary colors are especially appealing to children.)
- Newspaper
- Nontoxic lead-free latex or spray paint
- Glue (such as contact cement)
- Colored or patterned adhesive paper or craft tape (optional)

STEPS TO FOLLOW

1. Using a utility knife, cut a row of three holes in the lid of the box. Make each hole the diameter of a tube. Leave enough space between the holes for the napkin rings and your child's fingers.
2. Stuff the tubes with wadded-up newspaper to strengthen them. Be sure to push the newspaper far enough inside the tubes so that your child won't be tempted to pull it out.
3. Paint each tube to match a napkin ring color and insert a tube in each hole in the box.

4. Anchor the tubes to the bottom of the box with glue.
5. Tape the lid to the box.
6. If you like, decorate the box using latex or spray paint, colored or patterned adhesive paper, or craft tape.

ACTIVITY

Show your toddler how to stack the napkin rings on the spindles. Encourage the child to group them by color. Even toddlers who can't name the colors can still match items with like colors (the red rings with the red spindle).

VARIATION

In addition to stacking the napkin rings, your child can also use them for lacing activities— stringing them onto cord or plastic tubing. For toddlers, plastic aquarium air tube works well for lacing.

Tie one napkin ring to the end of a 12-inch piece of aquarium air tube. Then have your toddler hold a second napkin ring while you aim the loose end of the plastic tubing through the hole. Have your child let go of the second napkin ring, allowing it to drop down the tube and fall on top of the first napkin ring. Continue stringing the rest of the napkin rings in the same way.

THINGS TO TALK ABOUT

See the beginning of this chapter.

Shape Sorter Toy

WHAT YOU'LL NEED

○ Three containers, one for each shape (round, square, and triangular) the child will be sorting. The containers can be any of the following:

❑ Plastic storage bowls with lids
❑ Coffee cans with lids (Children enjoy using coffee cans because of the noise the sorting objects make when they hit the bottom.)
❑ Cardboard boxes with lids, such as frozen meat or shoe boxes
❑ Waxed ½-gallon cardboard milk or juice cartons (These cartons are sturdier than cardboard boxes.)
❑ Permanent marker or ballpoint pen

> **Safety note:** Pound down the inside rim of the coffee cans to avoid sharp edges.

○ A utility knife
○ Nontoxic lead-free latex or spray paint, colored or patterned adhesive paper, or craft tape (optional)

○ Round sorting objects that will not fit in the No Choke Testing Tube—Small Objects Tester (described in Part 2, *Tips for Making Toys*), such as:

❑ Small balls
❑ Round cookie cutters
❑ Beads (such as those children use for stringing)
❑ Thread spools
❑ Hair curlers (all with the same diameter)
❑ Napkin rings
❑ Cylinder-shaped building blocks
❑ Plastic Easter eggs

> ***Safety note:*** When using the small plastic Easter eggs, be sure to seal them shut with contact cement. When the eggs are opened, a half could become lodged in a child's mouth.

○ Square sorting objects, such as:

❑ ABC blocks
❑ Lumber scraps cut to match the size of the round sorting objects being used

> ***Safety note:*** Because of chemicals, avoid using scraps cut from pressure-treated lumber.

❑ Layers of corrugated cardboard glued together to a thickness of about 1 inch and cut into blocks using a hand saw
❑ Sponges cut into blocks with an electric carving knife or other sharp knife (To make cutting easier, make the sponges stiff by first wetting them and then letting them dry.)
❑ Bathtub blocks (Cut them with an electric carving knife to approximately the same size as the round sorting objects.)

> **Safety note:** Children who are still teething or who put objects in their mouths will need close supervision when playing with sponge or bathtub blocks. They may bite off pieces of the blocks.

○ Triangular sorting objects made from the materials described under square sorting objects (except for the ABC blocks)

STEPS TO FOLLOW

For each container with a lid:

1. On the container lid, trace one of the three shapes the child will be sorting—round, square, or triangular.
2. Cut the shape out of the lid using a utility knife and place the lid on the container. Check to see that only one type of shape can fit into the opening. (For example, make sure that the round sorting object will not fit into the square opening. That way, the activity will be self-correcting.)
3. If you like, decorate the container using latex or spray paint, colored or patterned adhesive paper, or craft tape. You can also decorate the wooden or cardboard shapes, using a different color for each type of shape.

For each milk or juice carton:

1. Cut off the top of the carton, where the two slanted sides are sealed.
2. Cut out the sides that were bent in. Then trim the remaining two flaps so that when you fold them in, they meet in the middle instead of overlapping.
3. Tape one of the flaps to the sides of the carton and leave the other to open and close freely, being sure the shapes fit through it. (Your child will be able to use this opening to empty the contents of the carton.)
4. Turn the carton on its side. In the middle of the carton, trace the shape of the object your child will be sorting.

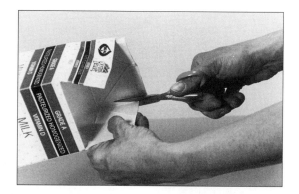
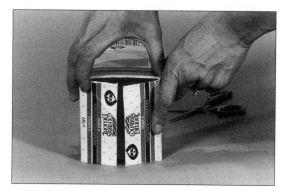

5. Cut out the shape. (If you're making multiple cartons, make certain that only one shape will fit into each opening. For example, make sure that the round shape will not fit into the square opening.)

6. If you like, decorate the carton with paint, adhesive paper, or craft tape. You can also decorate the wooden or cardboard shapes, using a different color for each type.

ACTIVITY

Demonstrate how to fit a shape into its opening. Once your child has placed all of the shapes in the container, empty it and start the game again.

Introduce the shape sorters one at a time, starting with the round one. Let your child master it before going on to the square. Once your child has mastered the square shape sorter, remove it before going on to the triangle. Children can become confused between squares and triangles since both have corners.

When your toddler has mastered working with the triangle, reintroduce the round shape, sorting the two shapes. Then sort the square and round shapes. Finally use the three containers side by side, letting your child choose the proper one for each shape. If you're using milk or juice cartons, tape them together (with the openings for removing shapes all facing the same direction).

Your toddler may have difficulty matching shapes to their openings. If so, try drawing an outline around the openings in the color that matches the shapes. This visual aid helps children who focus more on color than on shape. Later, as your child becomes more familiar with the shapes, you can make another lid without the color outlines.

VARIATION

Make a single shape sorter with all three shapes (circle, square, and triangle) cut into the lid. Cut one shape at a time and introduce only that shape to your toddler. When you introduce a new shape, place duct tape over existing openings and remove the shapes used with those openings. Then, as your child masters the new shape, remove the tape and reintroduce the previous shapes.

THINGS TO TALK ABOUT

See the beginning of this chapter.

Size Sorter Toy

WHAT YOU'LL NEED

○ Containers—the same as those listed for the shape sorter toy described earlier in this chapter (Either make new sorting containers following those instructions or use the same containers and only make new lids.)
○ A utility knife
○ Nontoxic lead-free latex or spray paint, colored or patterned adhesive paper, craft tape, stickers, or stamps (optional)
○ Sorting objects, such as:

  ❑ Large buttons
  ❑ Poker chips
  ❑ Plastic Easter eggs (large and small size)
  ❑ Jar lids in different sizes (A baby juice bottle lid, for example, is thick and small; a peel-off orange juice lid is thin and wide.)

> **Safety note:** Be sure to seal the small plastic Easter eggs with contact cement. When the eggs are opened, a half could become lodged in a child's mouth. Be sure to check each sorting item using the No-Choke Testing Tube—Small Objects Tester.

Steps to Follow

For each container used:

1. Cut an opening in the lid using a utility knife. Make the opening long enough and wide enough for the sorting object to pass through.
2. Place the lid on the container. When using multiple containers and sorting objects, check to see that only one sorting object fits into each opening. (In other words, make certain that the orange juice lid does not fit into the opening for the baby food jar lid. That way, the activity will be self-correcting.)
3. If you like, decorate the containers and sorting objects. (If you use stickers and stamps, make sure they're securely attached.)

Activity

Introduce your toddler to the size sorter toys one size at a time. Demonstrate how to fit the sorting object into the opening and let your child imitate you. Then empty the container and start the game again.

Let the child master each size sorting object before going on to a different one. Later, you can place two or three containers with different-sized openings side-by-side and have the child select the correct opening for each object.

Variations

Make a single size sorter toy with openings of several sizes cut into the same lid. Make one opening at a time and introduce it to your toddler. Each time you make a new opening, place opaque tape over the existing one(s) so that your child can practice with only one opening at a time. Then remove the tape and help your child sort two sizes and later three.

Things to Talk About

See the beginning of this chapter.

Sorting Hook Board

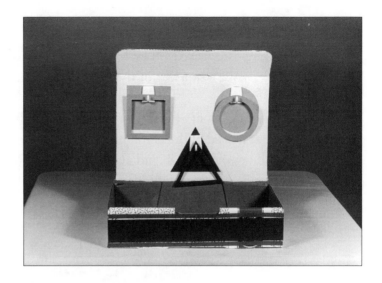

WHAT YOU'LL NEED

- A corrugated-cardboard box about 14 inches wide and 10 inches deep (A frozen meat box works well.)
- Scissors or a utility knife
- Three sheets of posterboard, each a different color
- Rubber cement
- Clear adhesive paper
- Small adhesive plastic hooks (available in hardware stores)
- Duct tape

STEPS TO FOLLOW

1. Make the sorting board using the corrugated-cardboard box:

   a. Cut out a circle, triangle, and square from the posterboard. Make each shape about 4 inches across and a different color.
   b. Use rubber cement to attach the three shapes to the inside of the box lid. Cover them with clear adhesive paper.

c. Attach a plastic hook near the top of each shape.

d. Support the board or box lid by leaning it against a wall or a piece of furniture. Or, if you choose, make a support for the back of the box lid:

1) Cut a rectangle out of heavy or corrugated cardboard about 3 or 4 inches wide and as long as the lid of the cardboard box.

2) Score the piece of cardboard about $1^1/2$ inches from the top and bend it.

3) Use duct tape to attach the top part of the cardboard rectangle, above the score, to the outside of the box lid.

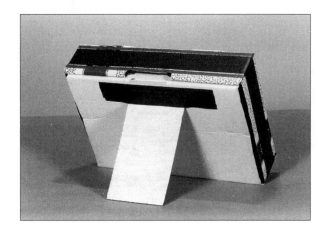

2. Make the three sets of sorting shapes: circles, triangles, and squares:

a. On one of the three sheets of posterboard draw four concentric circles. On another, draw four concentric squares. On the last, draw four concentric triangles. Each set of shapes should be about 4 inches across. Make these circles, squares, and triangles the same colors as the circle, square, and triangle you cut out earlier and attached to the box lid.

b. Cover both the front and the back of the concentric shapes with clear adhesive paper.

c. Cut out the shapes, discarding the middle one in each set. What remains are three circles, three squares, and three triangles in graduated sizes.

ACTIVITY

Show your toddler how to match the shapes cut out of posterboard to the pictures attached to the sorting hook board. Point out that there are two visual clues to use: shape and color. When your child finds a match, have him/her hang the cutout shape on the appropriate hook.

VARIATIONS

○ Cut sorting shapes out of opaque plastic report folders instead of posterboard. The plastic is durable and comes in different colors. However, it may be harder for some children to manipulate these shapes because the plastic is thin and flexible.

○ Have your child use the three versions of each cutout shape as nesting toys. For an explanation, see *Nesting Shapes* later in this chapter.

○ Use sets of graduated cookie cutters instead of making shapes from cardboard. Cookie cutters are available in a variety of shapes, such as ovals, circles, hearts, and stars.

THINGS TO TALK ABOUT

See the beginning of this chapter.

Mail Box Sorter

What You'll Need

- Cancelled stamps from mail or stickers
- A container that has a lid and is deep enough to allow the "letter" to drop to the bottom, such as a:

    - Plastic storage bowl
    - Plastic container from prepared cake frosting
    - Small cardboard box
    - Coffee can

> **Safety note:** Pound down the inside rim of the coffee can to avoid sharp edges.

    - Plastic container from baby wet wipes
    - A round oatmeal or cornmeal box (Although these boxes are a good size for this activity, the lids do not hold up well.)

○ Blue and red craft tape
○ Cardboard (primary colors)
○ Rubber cement
○ Clear adhesive paper or clear cellophane packaging tape

STEPS TO FOLLOW

1. Save cancelled stamps from mail.
2. Decorate the container with stripes of blue and red craft tape to make it look like a mail box.
3. Make a slit in the lid slightly longer than 2 inches.
4. Make "letters" by cutting the cardboard into 2-inch squares. Decorate them by gluing a cancelled stamp or sticker in the corner and by either drawing squiggly lines that look like writing or by writing your child's name and address on them.
5. Cover both sides of the "letters" with clear adhesive paper or clear cellophane packaging tape. Extend tape past edges on both sides and press to seal.

ACTIVITY

Show your toddler how to mail the letters by putting them through the slit in the top of the container lid. (Your child may have some difficulty because the opening in the mail box is narrow and the "letters" have corners, making it a challenge to insert them into the opening.) If this is difficult, put it away for a few weeks.

THINGS TO TALK ABOUT

As your child mails the letters, you can talk about what color they are and what pictures are on the stamps. For additional ideas, see the beginning of this chapter.

Nesting Containers

What You'll Need

○ Three to four containers that fit inside one another, such as mixing bowls, plastic storage containers, measuring cups, pans, juice containers, and coffee cans

Safety note: Pound down the inside rim of the coffee cans to avoid sharp edges.

Activity

Show your child how to fit the containers inside one another and how to turn them upside down and stack them on top of each other. Also demonstrate how to hide a smaller container by covering it with the next larger one.

Things to Talk About

See the beginning of this chapter.

Nesting Shapes

WHAT YOU'LL NEED

○ The cardboard shapes used with the sorting hook board activity described earlier in this chapter (circle, triangle, and square) or nesting cookie cutters (available in a variety of shapes, such as ovals, circles, hearts, and stars)

ACTIVITY

On a flat surface, have your child arrange a set of shapes by size, one inside the other. Also, show your toddler how to arrange a set of shapes in a row from biggest to smallest or from smallest to biggest.

THINGS TO TALK ABOUT

As your child plays with nesting shapes, you can discuss which is the biggest and which is the smallest. You can then take those shapes away and ask, "Of the ones that are left, which is the biggest? Which is the smallest?" For additional ideas, see the beginning of this chapter.

Puzzles

Overview

Puzzle play involves matching pieces to an outline, to another shape, or to a background. Most puzzles are made of wood, cardboard, plastic, or rubber; and they come in a wide range of ability levels.

Toddlers begin to enjoy puzzle play at about 18 to 24 months of age. They do best with simple wooden puzzles that have three or four separate shapes. These simple puzzles have no background and are usually thematic—related to water, zoo animals, farm animals, etc. Many times the puzzle pieces have knobs, making them easier for toddlers to manipulate.

The next step up in difficulty is puzzles with eight to ten pieces, each one a separate picture. These puzzles require a child to match the puzzle pieces to a picture underneath. Toddlers can have difficulty with this type of puzzle because the image underneath is often different from the image on the puzzle piece. While both images may be of squirrels, for example, each squirrel might be doing a different activity. This difference can be confusing to a young child. Also, few of these puzzles have pieces with knobs. Toddlers' fingers get in the way when they try to slide the pieces into place.

The next step up in complexity is a quantum leap. These puzzles, often made of wood or cardboard, show a complete picture divided into several differently shaped pieces that touch one another. Surrounding the picture is a border that contains visual clues to help the child decide where to place each puzzle piece. Completing this type of puzzle is difficult because it requires making many decisions. A child must decide which shapes, colors, and images match one another and the border.

Making your own puzzles is a way to help your toddler get enjoyment out of puzzle play while avoiding the frustrations. This chapter explains how to create puzzles that both reflect your child's interests and match his/her abilities.

Purpose

Playing with puzzles helps children develop skills they will later need for reading. Foremost among these skills is perceiving shapes, necessary for learning letters, words, and numbers. Much of our reading ability is based on this skill.

Puzzle play also helps children develop the following:

○ Finger dexterity (using the fingers to pick up puzzle pieces and put them in place)
○ Eye-hand coordination (aiming a puzzle piece at an opening and controlling the placement of the piece with the hands and eyes)
○ An understanding of one-to-one correspondence (seeing that an individual puzzle piece relates to a particular opening or to a matching picture, a basic element of math)
○ Visual discrimination (determining how objects are the same and different)

Things to Talk About

Some things to discuss as your child plays with puzzles are:

○ Directions: "This piece is at the top of the board; that one is at the bottom. This piece is next to the other one."
○ Spatial concepts: "This piece fits into this opening."
○ Shapes: "Why won't this piece fit into the opening? Are we trying to put a square shape into a round opening?"
○ Associations (how the pictures on the puzzle pieces are related): "Where do you think

you'd find these things? At the beach? On a picnic?" "What's happening in this picture? Can we tell a story about these animals?" (Children especially enjoy it when you make them part of the story by using their names, moving the puzzle pieces around as if they were puppets, and changing the tone of your voice.)

○ Body awareness (for puzzles that show people or animals): "Where do the feet go?" "Where should you put the tail?" "What's missing?"

Along with these topics, you can discuss how the shapes found in the puzzle (round, square, triangular, etc.) are also found all around you. This type of experience helps children realize that everything is made of shapes that come in different colors and sizes. When you relate playthings to the real world, you're teaching a child to generalize.

Recommendations

Some hints to keep in mind about puzzles are:

○ If a puzzle proves to be a little too hard for your child, help him/her finish it. You'll be teaching your child to complete a task and minimizing the child's frustration. Once the puzzle is completed, put it away for a while. You can try again later when you think your child might be ready for it. Playing with toys that are too difficult can teach children failure rather than success.

○ A way to organize puzzles is to assign a number, letter, or pattern to each. Write the symbol on the puzzle board and on the back of each piece. Then store the puzzle in a mesh fruit bag or a resealable plastic storage bag. (Keep the plastic bag out of the child's reach.) Stand the puzzle upright in a storage container, such as a magazine rack or a long narrow box. (If you stack the puzzles horizontally, your child might knock the pieces out by storing the puzzle upside down.)

Toys You Can Make:

○ Cookie Cutter Puzzle
○ Shape Puzzle Board

○ Matching Puzzle
○ Cut-Up Picture Puzzle
○ Body Awareness Puzzle
○ Flannel Board Puzzle

The instructions for making these toys follow.

Cookie Cutter Puzzle

WHAT YOU'LL NEED

- Two sheets of corrugated cardboard the same size—large enough to fit all of the cookie cutters with some space left over around the edges
- Three or four cookie cutters (You might want to use a set of related cookie cutters, such as holiday shapes, dinosaurs, or animals.)
- Nontoxic lead-free latex or spray paint
- Clear adhesive paper
- A utility knife
- Contact cement

STEPS TO FOLLOW

1. Paint one side of a sheet of corrugated cardboard.
2. Place the cookie cutters on the cardboard and trace the shapes.
3. Cover the cardboard sheet with clear adhesive paper.
4. Use a utility knife to cut out the shapes. You can save these shapes for future activities.
5. Make a backing for the puzzle by gluing the second piece of cardboard to the first with contact cement.

ACTIVITY

Use the cookie cutters as puzzle pieces. (Cookie cutters are useful for many other types of play as well, such as cutting out play dough shapes and tracing.)

THINGS TO TALK ABOUT

See the beginning of this chapter.

Shape Puzzle
Board

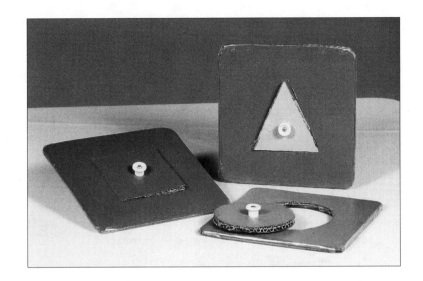

WHAT YOU'LL NEED

- ○ Contact cement
- ○ Two pieces of corrugated cardboard, each about 8 inches square
- ○ Nontoxic lead-free latex or spray paint
- ○ Clear adhesive paper
- ○ Permanent marker or ballpoint pen
- ○ A utility knife
- ○ A manual or electric drill
- ○ A small cabinet knob
- ○ Two washers (to fit the knob)
- ○ A nut (to fit the knob)

STEPS TO FOLLOW

1. Glue the two 8-inch squares of cardboard together.
2. Paint both sides of the corrugated cardboard in contrasting colors.
3. Cover both sides with clear adhesive paper.
4. Draw a shape (circle, triangle, or square) in the center of the cardboard, about 4 inches across, and cut it out.

5. Use a drill to make a small hole in the center of the shape where you will insert the cabinet knob. Before attaching the knob, find out which side of the shape your toddler prefers to use—the one that matches the background or the one that contrasts with it. For some children, contrasting colors help them to better see the opening in the puzzle. For others, matching a shape to a background of the same color is easier.

6. Secure the knob by placing a washer on each side of the hole and fastening the knob in the back with the nut.

ACTIVITY

Make a shape puzzle board for each shape: circle, square, and triangle. (Make sure that none of the shapes can fit into the openings on the other two boards.) Introduce the puzzles to your child one at a time with the same color sides facing up, allowing the child to master one before going on to another. With each, show your toddler how to grasp the puzzle piece by its handle and fit the piece into the opening. Later give your child the circle and square puzzles to solve. Then the circle and triangle puzzles, and lastly, present him and her with all three. Finally, introduce the boards' contrasting color sides in which to fit the shapes.

VARIATIONS

○ Make a shape puzzle board that contains all three shapes (circle, triangle, and square).
○ Add sensory stimulation to this activity by gluing textured fabric to the puzzle pieces instead of painting them. Tacky glue, available at craft stores, adheres well to fabric.
○ Make a simplified version of the shape puzzle board using lightweight cardboard, such as posterboard. For *each* shape (circle, square, and triangle) do the following:

   ❏ Draw the shape two times on a piece of colored board and cut out both.
   ❏ Draw the same shape in the center of a piece of white cardboard (or paper), making a heavy dark outline.
   ❏ Turn the white board over and on the back glue one of the colored cutout shapes in the center.
   ❏ Cover all surfaces with clear adhesive paper.

What you'll have are three white boards. Drawn on one side will be the outline of a shape. Glued to the other side will be a shape cut-out of colored paper.

To start the activity, have your child match the shapes by color—the cutout circle, square, and triangle with those glued to the back of each white board. Later, turn the white boards over so that the white outlined shapes are showing. See if your child can do the matching by outline only.

THINGS TO TALK ABOUT

See the beginning of this chapter.

Matching Puzzle

WHAT YOU'LL NEED

- Two identical pictures from coloring books, magazines, birthday cards, postcards, etc.
- Rubber cement
- Two sheets of posterboard the same size—slightly larger than the size of the pictures
- Clear adhesive paper
- A utility knife

STEPS TO FOLLOW

1. Mount each picture on a sheet of posterboard slightly larger than the picture.
2. Cover both pictures on both sides with clear adhesive paper.
3. Leave one picture whole and cut the other into two to four pieces.

ACTIVITY

There are two ways to conduct this activity. One is to have the child assemble the puzzle pieces on top of the whole picture. The other is to place the puzzle pieces and the whole picture side by side so that the child can refer to the whole image while assembling the pieces.

THINGS TO TALK ABOUT

See the beginning of this chapter.

Cut-Up Picture Puzzle

WHAT YOU'LL NEED

- A simple picture from a magazine, coloring book, catalog, postcard, or greeting card
- Scissors
- Posterboard
- Rubber cement
- Clear adhesive paper
- A utility knife

STEPS TO FOLLOW

1. Cut out the picture.
2. Mount it on posterboard cut slightly larger than the picture, using rubber cement.
3. Cover both sides of the picture with clear adhesive paper.
4. Using the utility knife, slice the picture in half.

ACTIVITY

Start by having your toddler match the two halves of the picture. As your child gets better at this activity, cut the picture into more pieces.

THINGS TO TALK ABOUT

See the beginning of this chapter.

Body
Awareness
Puzzle

WHAT YOU'LL NEED

- An easily identifiable picture of a person or animal that contains either the face or the entire body outline
- A sheet of posterboard slightly larger than the size of the picture
- Rubber cement
- Clear adhesive paper
- A utility knife

STEPS TO FOLLOW

1. Using the rubber cement, glue the magazine picture to the sheet of corrugated cardboard.
2. Cover the picture and back side of the board with clear adhesive paper.
3. Cut out the picture so that it's an outline of a face or body.
4. Make the puzzle pieces by cutting the picture into three or four identifiable segments (such as the head, the upper torso and limbs, and the lower torso and limbs).

ACTIVITY

Help your child identify the body parts shown on each of the puzzle pieces and discuss where those parts go in relation to the whole body. Then help the child place the puzzle pieces in the proper position.

THINGS TO TALK ABOUT

See the beginning of this chapter.

Flannel Board Puzzle

WHAT YOU'LL NEED

- A box with a lid (such as a cigar, meat, or gift box), a sheet of corrugated cardboard, or a piece of wood (about 12 × 14 inches)
- Flannel fabric (You can buy it new at a fabric store or cut up old flannel clothing, such as a shirt or nightgown.)
- Duct tape, rubber cement, or staples
- Any of the following:

  - One or more pieces of felt fabric and a pen or permanent marker

> **Safety note:** Avoid using felt puzzle pieces and permanent markers with children who are still teething or who put objects in their mouths. Felt pulls apart easily, and permanent markers are toxic.

  - Fabric softener sheets and a pen or permanent marker (These sheets are a good alternative to felt. Drawing on them with markers is easier than it is on felt, and the sheets don't stretch and pull apart the way felt does.)

❑ Pictures cut out of books, magazines, or coloring books (When using pictures, you'll also need a sheet of thin cardboard, clear adhesive paper, and a strip of sandpaper or self-adhesive Velcro.)

STEPS TO FOLLOW

1. Make the flannel board by covering the inside of the box lid, the sheet of corrugated cardboard, or the piece of wood with flannel and securing the flannel with duct tape, rubber cement, or staples. (If you use staples, be sure to place heavy tape over them for safety.)
2. Make the puzzle pieces in one of two ways:

❑ Use the pen or permanent marker to draw a picture on the felt or fabric softener sheets and cut the picture into pieces. The picture can be a person, animal, geometric shape, or other familiar object. The felt pieces will adhere to the flannel.

❑ Cut a picture out of a book, magazine, or coloring book and use rubber cement to mount it on thin cardboard. Cover the picture with clear adhesive paper and cut it into two to four identifiable pieces. Glue a strip of sandpaper or attach a strip of self-adhesive Velcro to the back of each piece. Both the sandpaper and Velcro will adhere to the flannel.

ACTIVITY

Show your toddler how to assemble the puzzle pieces on the flannel board. This activity is the hardest of all the puzzle activities described in this chapter. If your toddler has difficulty with it, save the activity until the child is a little older.

VARIATIONS

○ Use whole pictures (not cut into puzzle pieces) of people, animals, and objects on the flannel board to tell stories or to talk about colors and shapes.

○ Attach strip magnets to the back of the whole picture shapes mounted on cardboard. (The magnets are sold in rolls at craft stores and have an adhesive backing on one side.) Let your child stick the shapes on the refrigerator or other metal surface.

THINGS TO TALK ABOUT

See the beginning of this chapter.

Pegboard Toys

Overview

Pegboards come in all sizes. They can be made of wood, plastic, rubber, and even cardboard boxes. Commercially, they are available alone or combined with other toys, such as chalkboards. With all types of pegboards, the play activity is the same—sticking the peg into a narrow-fitting hole, leaving part of the peg exposed.

Pegboard play seems to come naturally to children at around 18 to 20 months of age. It's an activity that's easy to do and self-explanatory. Children see the holes and automatically want to stick the pegs in.

Purpose

Playing with pegboards helps develop the following:

- Finger dexterity. Children pick up the pegs and fit them into the holes.
- Eye-hand coordination. In placing pegs into openings, children aim at a target and control its placement with their hands and eyes.
- Spatial awareness and directionality. Children move the pegs in and out of holes and place the pegs in various locations on the pegboard (top, bottom, sides).

○ Patterning skills. Children can learn to recognize simple patterns that adults make with colored pegs and to duplicate the patterns. These skills help prepare children for later learning in school.

○ Goal setting. Children identify tasks on the pegboard they want to complete, such as making a line of pegs, and work to complete them.

THINGS TO TALK ABOUT

Some things to discuss as your child plays with pegboards and pegs are:

○ Colors: "Here's a red peg. There's a blue one."

○ Directions: "Let's put this peg at the top of the board." "Can you put yours at the side of the board?" (Children in this age group are not yet ready for left and right.)

○ Spatial concepts: "The red peg is in the hole. You took the blue peg out of the hole. See if you can put the red peg between the two blue pegs."

○ Numbers: "One peg, two pegs, three pegs in the holes."

Toddlers' main focus in playing with pegboards is getting the pegs into the holes. A secondary interest might be creating or duplicating simple patterns with different-colored pegs; for example, a red peg, a blue peg, and a red peg arranged in a horizontal row, in a vertical row, or in a diagonal row. Purposely creating shapes with the pegs, such as circles, squares, and triangles, is probably beyond a toddler's capabilities at this point.

Toys You Can Make:

○ Clothespin Pegboard

○ Golf Tee Pegboard

○ Picture Pegboard

○ Copycat Pegboard

The instructions for making these toys follow.

Clothespin Pegboard

WHAT YOU'LL NEED

- A thin cardboard gift box (The box must be low enough to keep the clothespins from falling through the holes and into the box. The bottom of the box should stop the clothespins when they are about halfway through the holes.)
- Colored duct tape
- Wooden clothespins with rounded tops
- Manicure scissors
- Nontoxic lead-free spray paint

STEPS TO FOLLOW

1. Tape the box lid shut with colored duct tape. (If you plan to use this toy for traveling, omit this step. You can store the clothespins inside the box.)
2. Draw the rows of pegboard holes on the lid, using a clothespin turned upside down to trace them.
3. Cut out the holes using manicure scissors.
4. Spray paint the clothespins in different colors.

ACTIVITY

Show your child how to insert the upside-down clothespins into the holes. This pegboard is the most basic of those described in this chapter and is well suited to young toddlers.

VARIATIONS

o Instead of using a box as a pegboard, use a cardboard egg carton turned upside down. For instructions on how to make this toy, see *Clothespin Hammering* in the chapter *Pounding Toys*.

o Instead of clothespins, use any of the following:

❑ Smooth hair curlers
❑ Cylinder-shaped blocks that come with building block sets
❑ Sections of the cardboard tube that comes on pants hangers from the cleaners

(Keep in mind that the younger the child, the larger the pegs should be—but still small enough for a toddler to grasp.)

THINGS TO TALK ABOUT

See the beginning of this chapter.

Golf Tee Pegboard

WHAT YOU'LL NEED

- A sturdy box at least 3 inches deep (A mailing box or frozen meat box, usually white and corrugated, works best.)
- Pencil
- Ruler
- Nontoxic lead-free latex or spray paint, colored or patterned adhesive paper, or craft tape (optional)
- Jumbo golf tees approximately 3 inches long (Most commercially sold pegs are too small to be safe for very young children and are also difficult for them to manipulate.)

STEPS TO FOLLOW

1. Use the pencil and ruler to draw a grid on the top of the box. The squares of the grid should be at least 1 inch square.
2. Poke holes where the lines intersect.
3. If you choose, decorate the box with paint, adhesive paper, or craft tape.

ACTIVITY

Show your toddler how to poke the golf tees into the holes. When your child is finished playing with this pegboard, you can store the golf tees inside the box.

> *Safety note:* Children who put things in their mouths require close supervision when playing with golf tees. A safer toy for these children is the preceding one, clothespin pegboard.

VARIATIONS

o Use other items in place of golf tees for pegs, such as:

  ❑ Bicycle spoke covers
  ❑ Straws
  ❑ Sections of the cardboard tube that comes on pants hangers from the cleaners

  Cut each of these into 3-inch pieces.

o Instead of poking the golf tees all the way through the cardboard, just poke them in part way and let your child hammer them in the rest of the way. For additional information, see the *Golf Tee Hammering* toy in the chapter *Pounding Toys*.

THINGS TO TALK ABOUT

See the beginning of this chapter.

Picture
Pegboard

WHAT YOU'LL NEED

- A piece of lightweight cardboard or posterboard the same size as the pegboard
- A pegboard (See the instructions for the *Clothespin Pegboard* or *Golf Tee Pegboard* earlier in this chapter.)
- A marker or crayon
- Clear adhesive paper
- A hand drill or ice pick

STEPS TO FOLLOW

1. Place the cardboard facedown over the pegboard, turn the pegboard upside down, and trace the holes onto the cardboard.
2. Draw a simple shape on the face of the cardboard so that there are holes along the outline of the shape. (You might try a triangle, a square, or a house shape.) For a toddler, you only need about six holes in the picture.
3. Cover both sides of the cardboard.
4. Cut out the holes using a hand drill or an ice pick. The tool you use must be sharp, or it will shred the cardboard.

ACTIVITY

Introduce your toddler to the activity by holding the cardboard and letting the child put the pegs into the holes in the picture. After your child has practiced for a little while, remove the pegs and place the picture on the pegboard. Line the picture up over the holes by inserting the first two pegs. Then let your toddler do the rest.

VARIATIONS

○ Using the *Clothespin Hammering* or *Golf Tee Hammering* toys (described in the chapter *Pounding Toys*), have your child take a crayon or watercolor marker and connect holes on the box. Then have the child follow the design with pegs.

○ For older toddlers, cut out pictures instead of drawing them. The steps to follow are:

   ❑ Select a picture from a magazine, coloring book, greeting card, or postcard. (Pictures from magazines or coloring books should be mounted on lightweight cardboard with rubber cement.) The picture should have simple lines, with a predominant geometric shape.

   ❑ Cover both sides of the picture with clear adhesive paper.

   ❑ Place the picture faceup and lay the pegboard facedown on top of it.

   ❑ Using a pen, make a mark where each hole in the picture should be. Make only six to ten holes, following the basic outline of the picture.

   ❑ Use the hand drill or ice pick to make the holes.

   ❑ Place the picture on the pegboard faceup and insert the first two pegs to line it up for your toddler. Then let your child do the rest.

   When your child is older, you can also use these pictures for sewing cards.

○ Give your toddler a piece of paper or cardboard cut to the size of the pegboard and have the child draw a picture on it. Then follow the steps above to make the holes in the picture and place it on the pegboard.

THINGS TO TALK ABOUT

See the beginning of this chapter.

Copycat Pegboard

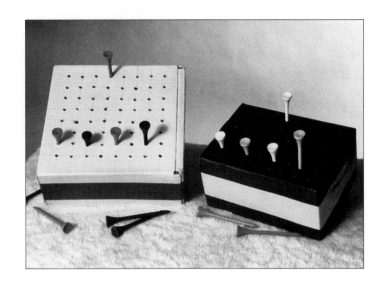

○ Two pegboards and two sets of colored pegs. (See the instructions for the *Clothespin Pegboard* or *Golf Tee Pegboard* earlier in this chapter.)

If you make one pegboard larger than the other, the smaller one, along with the golf tees, will fit inside the larger for storage.

ACTIVITY

Both you and your child will have a pegboard and a set of colored pegs. Start the activity by creating a simple pattern with the pegs and challenge your toddler to copy it. For example, you might make a horizontal line with three pegs: a red one, a blue one, and a red one. Then you might ask, "Can you make a row of pegs that looks like this?"

Keep the patterns simple, with no more than three or four pegs and two colors. Also, vary the placement of the patterns. Put them at the top, the bottom, and the sides of the board.

VARIATION

Play the picture pegboard game described in the previous activity. Both you and your child will have a pegboard, pegs, and identical pictures mounted on your pegboards. Challenge your child to insert pegs into the picture in the same places that you do.

THINGS TO TALK ABOUT

See the beginning of this chapter.

Visual Tracking Toys and Activities

Overview

The toys and activities in this category are all quite different. What they have in common is that they all involve movement of some type, such as bubbles floating through the air or flashlight beams moving across a dark room. This movement attracts the attention of children of all ages and causes their eyes to follow the movement through space. The ability of the eyes to work together to follow movement is called visual tracking.

Purpose

Visual tracking is an ability toddlers will later need for reading. The eye muscles must work together, moving from left to right, to identify letters, numbers, words, and sentences. Additional information about the purpose of the toys and activities in this chapter is included with the description of each.

Toys You Can Make and Things You Can Do:

○ Ball Roller Coaster

○ Lid Track
○ Pegboard Maze
○ Bubble Play
○ Flashlight Play

The instructions for these toys and activities follow.

Ball Roller Coaster

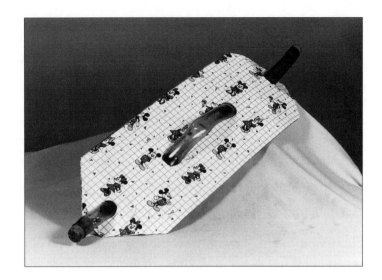

What You'll Need

- A large rectangular piece of cardboard (approximately 26 × 8 inches)
- A utility knife or manicure scissors (Manicure scissors work well for cutting circular holes since the blades are curved.)
- A piece of flexible vinyl tubing 34 to 36 inches long and 1 inch in diameter (available at hardware stores)
- Two corks approximately 1 inch in diameter
- Glue (Contact cement works best.)
- Objects small enough to fit easily inside the tubing, such as beads, bells, cake sprinkles, or marbles. While objects this size are small enough to fit in the No Choke Testing Tube—Small Objects Tester (described in Part 2, *Tips for Making Toys*), they will be permanently enclosed in the toy and unavailable to your child.

Steps to Follow

1. Make four evenly spaced holes in the cardboard, extending from top to bottom. The holes should be slightly larger than 1 inch in diameter.
2. Lace the tubing through the holes. Start with the highest hole and leave a section of

tubing extended at the top. Avoid making any sharp bends in the tubing that would prevent the objects from rolling through. Also leave some tubing extended at the bottom.

3. Insert a cork completely in the bottom end of the tubing, shaving if necessary to make it fit. Use glue to secure it in place.
4. Insert the objects in the tube.
5. Seal the top end of the tubing by inserting the other cork and securing it with glue.
6. Cut off any cork that extends beyond the tube's ends.

ACTIVITY

Show your toddler how to turn the toy to make the objects inside roll from one end to the other. Point out that the way the toy is turned affects the way the objects move through the tubing. Your child can manipulate the toy so that the objects move in different ways. They can go from top to bottom, stop in the middle, go fast and then slow, and so forth.

VARIATIONS

○ Make more than one tube. For contrast, you might use a combination of objects, such as a bead, a marble, and a homemade ball made of wadded-up aluminum foil. Point out to your child how the different objects move through the tubing in different ways.
○ Fill the tubing with water and add items to the water to make it more interesting for your child to watch, such as toothpicks, pieces of Styrofoam, glitter, or food coloring.
○ Fill the tubing with a mixture of oil and water. Point out to your child how the two liquids remain separate.

PURPOSE

In addition to visual tracking, manipulating the Ball Roller Coaster develops upper-arm strength and control. It also demonstrates two concepts for children. One is cause and effect. They see that by performing an action, they can produce a predictable outcome. The other concept is gravity. Slanting the Ball Roller Coaster downward causes its contents to move to the bottom of the toy.

THINGS TO TALK ABOUT

Some questions to ask as your child plays with this toy are:

o "What happens if you hold the toy sideways?" "Do the things inside move?"
o "What happens if you tilt it a little toward the floor?" "If you tilt it a lot toward the floor, will the things inside move faster?"
o "If you turn the toy quickly back and forth, will the things inside go all the way from end to end or stop in the middle and go back again?"

Lid Track

What You'll Need

- A shoe box
- A utility knife
- A narrow cardboard tube (the type that comes with fabric softener or plastic wrap)
- A ruler
- Container lids in small and/or large sizes (Plastic storage container lids and peel-off metal lids from frozen orange juice cans work well.)
- Nontoxic lead-free spray paint or stickers to decorate the lids

Steps to Follow

1. Remove the top of the shoe box. Then cut a notch out of the upper edge of one of the wide sides of the box. This notch, which will support the cardboard tube, should be the same width as the tube.
2. In the cardboard tube, cut a narrow slit from top to bottom using the ruler and utility knife. The slit should be wide enough to allow the lids to roll down the tube.
3. Position the tube in the notch. During play, you can change the incline of the tube, making the slope steeper or more gradual.

4. Place the box top underneath the box for stability.

5. If you like, decorate the container lids with spray paint or stickers. You might also decorate the box and tube.

ACTIVITY

Show your child how to position a lid at the top of the track (the cardboard tube) and release the lid so that it rolls down and onto the play surface. Point out when the lid rolls in a different direction as it leaves the track. If you're using both large and small lids, compare the distance each rolls. You can mark their stopping points with masking tape or with toys or other objects.

Try placing something underneath the lower end of the tube to change the incline and the drop from the end of the tube to the play surface. Point out the effect that such changes have on the way the lid rolls and lands. When you finish playing with this toy, store the tube and lids inside the box.

VARIATION

Instead of using a box to support the cardboard tubing, lean the tube against something, such as a wall, pillow, or piece of furniture. This will make the tube less stable and affect the way the lids roll.

PURPOSE

Along with improving visual tracking, this toy helps children develop finger dexterity and eye-hand coordination. It also gives children a simple introduction to the concepts of gravity, velocity, and incline.

The lid track demonstrates cause and effect as well. Every time a child changes something, such as the incline of the track, there's an identifiable result. The toy also encourages anticipation. As children release a lid at the top of the track, they anticipate which way it will go when it leaves the track.

THINGS TO TALK ABOUT

Some questions to ask as your child plays with this toy are:

- ○ "By moving the track this way, can we make the lid go faster or slower?"
- ○ "How far did the lid roll?" (You can mark it with tape or an object on the floor.)
- ○ "Which way did the lid go at the bottom—straight ahead or to the side?"
- ○ "Which lid goes faster—the big one or the little one?"

Pegboard Maze

WHAT YOU'LL NEED

○ A piece of flexible coated wire (8-strand electrical wire). The piece should be about 8 feet long if you want three wires on the maze or longer if you want four.

○ Wire cutters

○ A pegboard, about eight holes square, made from a cardboard box (See instructions for the *Golf Tee Pegboard* in the chapter *Pegboard Toys.*)

○ Objects to manipulate, such as large beads, spools, plastic practice golf balls, bathtub blocks, and the wooden shapes used with the shape-sorting toys described in the chapter *Stacking, Sorting, and Nesting Toys* (You'll need to drill a hole through the bathtub blocks and the wooden shapes.)

○ Masking tape

STEPS TO FOLLOW

1. Bend each length of wire to the approximate shape you want before cutting it. Allow an extra one to two inches at both ends for inserting the wire in the pegboard and securing it. For a three-wire maze, suggested lengths to cut are 34 inches, 27 inches, and 23 inches.

2. Attach two to four objects (beads, spools, etc.) to each wire.

3. For each wire, insert the two ends into holes on opposite sides of the pegboard. Push each end of the wire through both the top and bottom of the box. Then turn the box upside down and secure the ends of the wire by bending each into an "L" shape.

ACTIVITY

This activity has two parts. One is moving the objects around the wires—pushing them up the slopes and watching them slide down. The other part is helping design and redesign the toy. Although you'll need to position the wires in new locations, your child can tell you where to begin and end the wire and how to bend it. (Children have more pride and interest in something they help to create.)

VARIATION

Make only the holes you need in the top of the box. Three well-spaced holes along each of two opposite sides of the box top will work well. Insert the wires and secure them following the instructions given earlier in Step 3.

PURPOSE

Along with improving a child's visual tracking ability, moving objects around the pegboard maze helps develop the following:

○ Eye-hand coordination
○ Upper-arm control
○ A sense of spatial awareness (where objects are in space)
○ Directionality (which way objects are moving)
○ An understanding of the effects of gravity and velocity (as children push objects up the wires and watch them slide down)
○ Color and shape recognition
○ An understanding of numbers (the number of objects strung on each wire)

In addition, playing with the pegboard maze encourages crossing the midline—body control that involves reaching and grasping across the midline of the body. Taking part in designing and redesigning the maze encourages creativity.

THINGS TO TALK ABOUT

Some things to discuss as your child plays with this toy are:

○ Shapes: "The ball is round, and the bead is square."
○ Sizes: "This bead is bigger than that one."
○ Colors: "Where is the red bead? Where's the blue one?"
○ Directions: "Let's push the shapes up the slide. Now let's make them go down."
○ Numbers: "That's one spool going down the slide. That's two spools. . . ."
○ Spatial concepts: "Would you like this wire to go over that one?" "Should we make that wire go under the other one?"

You can also give your child a simple introduction to the concepts of gravity and velocity. Point out that: "We have to push the bead up the slide, but it goes down all by itself." Discuss the effects of changing the slant of the wire: "The taller we make the slide, the faster the spool will go." Explain that the size of the object affects its speed: "The bigger the bead, the faster it goes."

Bubble Play

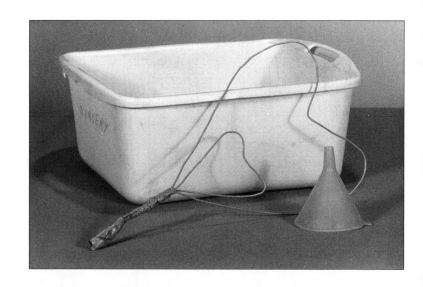

WHAT YOU'LL NEED

- Baby shampoo (Generic brands work well.)
- Water
- Sugar
- A low, wide container for the bubble solution, such as a plastic tub, cake pan, or any of the other containers listed in the chapter *Fill and Dump Activities*
- For indoor bubble play, something that a child can stand on without slipping, such as a rubber bath mat, a nonskid pad that goes under rugs, foam carpet padding, or a towel (A problem with towels is that they can bunch up as the child moves around.)
- Bubble blowers:

  - A funnel (Dip the wide part in the bubble solution and blow through the small part.)
  - Cylindrical containers, such as cans or small plastic bottles, with the tops removed and holes drilled in the bottom (Dip the open end of the container in the bubble solution and blow through the small hole at the opposite end.)
  - A kitchen baster without the bulb (Dip the open end of the baster in the bubble solution and blow through the small hole at the opposite end.)

○ Bubble wands:

  ❑ Plastic rings that hold six-packs of canned beverages (Dip them into the bubble solu-
     tion and wave them.)
  ❑ A store-bought bubble wand
  ❑ A coat hanger wand (Form plastic-coated coat hangers into various shapes, such as a
     heart or diamond. For safety, bend in the hook portion of the hanger and cover it with
     duct tape.)
  ❑ A slotted spoon from the kitchen (Dip it in the solution and hold it out while you turn
     in a circle.)

○ Giant bubble makers (for outdoor bubble play):

  ❑ A round cake pan with a removable bottom (Remove the bottom of the pan, hold on
     to the rim, and dip the pan in the solution. Then slowly turn in a circle.)
  ❑ An embroidery hoop
  ❑ A fabric triangle made from the following:

     △ A piece of bias tape about ¼ inch wide and 4 feet long
     △ A drill
     △ Two ¼-inch dowel rods, each about 1 foot long
     △ A large bead

(Lay out the bias tape in the shape of an isosceles triangle—one with two equal sides.
Position one of the equal sides at the top of the triangle. Drill a hole near the top of each
dowel rod large enough to pass the bias tape through. Secure a dowel rod at each corner of
the top of the triangle. Do this by threading the bias tape through the hole in each dowel rod
and knotting it in place. Secure the bead at the third corner of the triangle in the same way,
by knotting it.

To make bubbles, grasp the two dowel rods, bring them together, and dip the fabric triangle in the bubble solution. Then lift up the triangle and pull the dowel rods apart. Walk holding the triangle out to the side or let the wind catch the bubble and blow it.)

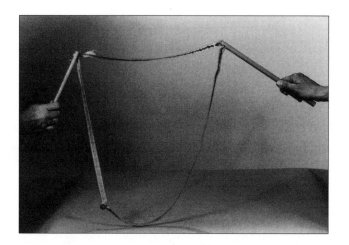

Steps to Follow

To make the bubble solution:

1. Mix 3 ounces of baby shampoo with each cup of water used.
2. Add 2 tablespoons of sugar per cup of water.

When you mix the bubble solution, avoid making suds, which interfere with the bubbles. If you see suds on top of the solution, skim them off.

Activity

Bubble play can be an indoor as well as an outdoor activity. If you're doing it indoors, place your child and the container of bubble solution on a piece of absorbent material that will not slip. Another alternative is to give your child a small container of bubbles to play with in the bathtub. For either indoor or outdoor play, fill your container about halfway with bubble solution.

You might begin bubble play by showing your toddler ways to play with bubbles: waving the wand to make a bubble come off, catching bubbles in his/her hand, poking them as they fall, clapping them, stepping on them, fanning them with a piece of paper, using a wand to catch one bubble on top of another. Next, you can teach your child how to make bubbles using wands and blowers.

Blowing bubbles is usually difficult for a toddler. Begin by blowing a bubble yourself and catching it on a wand. Then show your child how to blow the bubble off the wand. Doing it this way is much easier for a toddler because it requires less control than doing the initial blowing.

PURPOSE

Along with encouraging visual tracking, bubble play also helps develop eye-hand coordination (both in making the bubbles and in playing with them). In addition, blowing bubbles helps promote breath control, which aids in the development of good speech.

THINGS TO TALK ABOUT

Some things to discuss as your child plays with bubbles are:

○ Size: "These bubbles are little; that one is big."
○ Quantity: "Look how many bubbles we made." "This time we only made a few bubbles." "Let's count the bubbles—one . . . two . . ."
○ Colors: "What colors do you see in the bubbles?" "Does it look like a rainbow?"
○ Directions: "The wind is taking the bubbles up; it's blowing them down." "Are the bubbles going up high? Down low?"
○ Movement and body awareness (the child's body relationship to the bubble and control of it): "Look how fast you got to that bubble." "You caught it in your hand."
○ Spatial concepts: "There's a bubble on the floor, behind your foot."

Flashlight Play

WHAT YOU'LL NEED

○ A flashlight small enough for a toddler to grasp and easy enough for a toddler to turn on and off (Most flashlights, even those made for children, are too big and heavy for toddlers to use. Also, they usually have switches that toddlers are unable to work, especially with one hand. It's best to buy toddlers their own small flashlight that turns on by pressing a button. A brand well suited to toddlers is the Mini Tuff Lite by Garrity, shown above. It's the right size for a young child to hold and is easy to turn on and off. The child can stand the flashlight bulb side down and, with one finger, push the on/off button located at the opposite end. Another advantage of this flashlight is its rubber coating, which minimizes damage if a child throws it. Also, the flashlight requires only two AA batteries.)

> *Safety note:* If your child tends to remove batteries, use a sticky tape or a small amount of glue to keep the child from opening the flashlight.

ACTIVITIES

Two flashlight games to play with your child are:

○ Spot It: Call out the name of an object in the room, such as a piece of furniture, and have your child shine the light on it. Or shine your light on an object and ask your child to identify it. ("Look where my light is. What do you call that?")

○ Flashlight Tag: Using your own flashlight, move the beam across the walls and ceiling and have your child try to catch it with his/her own beam. When you get caught, you and your child reverse roles.

PURPOSE

Flashlight games help develop long-distance eye-hand coordination—the type needed in sports skills, such as throwing, catching, and hitting a ball. It gives children the opportunity to aim at objects across the room instead of immediately in front of them. An added benefit of the Spot It game is that it helps to build a child's vocabulary.

THINGS TO TALK ABOUT

Some things to discuss as your child plays with flashlights are:

○ Size: "When my flashlight is close to the wall, the dot is small. When I move away, the dot gets bigger."

○ Speed: "Your light is moving fast. I can make mine move slowly."

○ Directions: "My dot of light is up on the ceiling. Can you move your light up to the ceiling?"

Messy Play Activities

Overview

The messy play activities described in this chapter involve recipes for making finger paint, play dough, bubbles, and ink with ingredients generally found around the house. These activities engage children in manipulative play and provide tactile and visual experiences.

Messy play activities begin to appeal to children between 12 and 18 months of age. The activities are loosely structured and allow children to do as they choose—even, in some cases, to eat the play materials. Children at this age do not yet have a creative purpose for playing with these materials. For example, they do not deliberately set out to make a dog out of play dough. That comes at a later age.

Purpose

Messy play activities provide sensory stimulation not found with other types of play. In addition, they help children develop eye-hand coordination as well as an understanding of cause and effect. With this type of play, children can see the direct effects or products of their movements and actions. For additional information on the benefits of this type of play, see the descriptions of each activity in this chapter.

Things You Can Make:

- Food Finger Paints
- Edible Play Dough
- Make-Your-Own Ink
- Homemade Bubbles

The instructions for making these follow.

Food Finger Paints

WHAT YOU'LL NEED

○ Any of the following:

  ❑ Pudding or fruit-flavored gelatin (When making these, add ¼ to ½ cup of cornstarch to the hot water to make the mixture thicker and better for painting. Before using either the pudding or gelatin, let it stand at room temperature to soften.)
  ❑ Diluted frosting mix
  ❑ Yogurt

○ A cookie sheet or thin pizza pan
○ Objects for making designs, such as a tongue depressor or comb (It's a good idea to avoid using eating utensils in order to keep eating and playing with food separate in your child's mind. You might even want to avoid telling your child that the finger paint is food.)

ACTIVITY

Place a small amount of food finger paint on a cookie sheet or pizza pan and demonstrate how to move it around and how to make patterns in it with your fingers. Then demonstrate how to paint using one hand and two hands, how to make a hand print, how to make lines by clawing through the finger paint with your fingers, and how to use objects, such as a comb, to make patterns in it.

Variations

○ For a child who doesn't enjoy messy hands, put a special finger paint mixture inside a resealable plastic freezer bag. (The one-gallon size works well.) Make the mixture out of various colorful food items, such as mayonnaise, ketchup, and mustard, using about one tablespoon of each. Once you fill the bag, squeeze out the air, seal the bag, and place it on the play surface. Then show your toddler how to manipulate the bag by pushing on it to combine the colors and move the contents around.

○ For finger paint that is still edible but less recognizable as food, mix two parts flour and three parts water. Add a small amount of food coloring or fruit juice to the water for color or a small amount of extract, such as vanilla, almond, spearmint, or peppermint, for scent.

Purpose

Finger painting helps children develop strength in their fingers and hands. For additional information on the benefits of messy play activities, see the section entitled *Purpose* at the beginning of this chapter.

Things to Talk About

Some things to discuss as your toddler finger paints are:

○ The texture of the finger paint (mushy, watery)
○ The temperature of the finger paint (warm, cold)
○ The types of lines your child makes (straight, curved, swirling)
○ The number of lines
○ The shapes your child makes (circle, square, triangle)
○ Where your child is drawing lines (at the top, bottom, or sides of the cookie sheet)

Edible Play Dough

What You'll Need

o Powdered milk (as much as the quantity of play dough you want)
o Peanut butter
o Objects a child can poke or press into the play dough, such as:

  ❑ Tongue depressors (available at a doctor's office or at craft stores), which make good substitute knives
  ❑ Cookie cutters
  ❑ Birthday candle holders (safe only for children who no longer put things in their mouths)
  ❑ Combs
  ❑ A piece of dowel rod or a cylindrical block to use as a rolling pin (You may have to do the rolling since children this age are usually unable to do it themselves.)
  ❑ Nesting shapes, such as cups or stars
  ❑ A potato masher
  ❑ Hair curlers

○ Objects for pounding on the play dough, such as a wooden meat mallet or a toy hammer (Toy hammers with designs on the pounding end are commercially available for this purpose.)

Steps to Follow

1. Add peanut butter, a little at a time, to the powdered milk, pressing the mixture with a spoon.
2. When the mixture gets too difficult to stir with a spoon, use your hands.
3. Keep adding peanut butter until the mixture has a soft, pliable consistency.

Activity

Seat your child at a table and demonstrate how to play with edible play dough. Among the activities toddlers enjoy are:

○ Chopping a thin, long roll of play dough into pieces (You'll need to form the roll for your child.)
○ Pressing cookie cutters into the play dough (You'll need to flatten the play dough and show your child how to use the cookie cutters. At this age, children don't know how to make separate shapes. They make multiple impressions, one on top of another.)
○ Pretend play (You can help develop your child's interest in pretend play by using the toy cooking and eating utensils to make pretend play dough food and to serve pretend play dough meals.)

Variation

For play dough that's still edible but less tasty and nutritious, mix the following:

○ One cup of flour
○ A half cup of salt
○ Two teaspoons of cream of tartar

○ About one cup of water (For color, add food coloring to the water. For both color and scent, add a powdered fruit drink mix or add food coloring plus an extract, such as vanilla, almond, spearmint, or peppermint.)

Cook the mixture over a low flame, scraping the sides of the pan. When the mixture thickens and hardens at the sides of the pan, remove it from the heat and let it cool slightly. Then coat your hands with oil and knead the play dough. Store it in plastic wrap or in an airtight container. This mixture does not need refrigeration.

PURPOSE

Manipulating play dough helps children build strength in their fingers and hands. It can also be an outlet for stress. Children can release tension by using their hands or an object to pound on play dough. For additional information on the benefits of messy play activities, see the section entitled *Purpose* at the beginning of this chapter.

THINGS TO TALK ABOUT

Some things to discuss as your child plays with play dough are:

○ What the child is making with the play dough (its shape, size, etc.)
○ What tools the child is using to work with the play dough
○ What portion of the flattened play dough the child is working on (top, sides, bottom, center)
○ The consistency and texture of the play dough (stiff, rubbery, squishy, lumpy, hard)
○ The play dough's form and shape (rolled into a ball, flattened, made into a long skinny roll, made into pretend food)
○ The color of the play dough ("What happens when we mix these two colors together?")
○ The scent of the play dough (if one has been added to the recipe)

You can also present challenges to your child, such as: "Can you flatten the play dough?" "Can you press the dog cookie cutter next to the cat cookie cutter?"

Make-Your-Own Ink

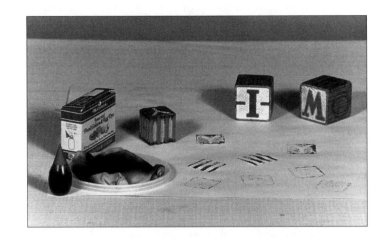

- Ink made from any of the following:

  - A mixture of either dish washing soap or white glue—as much as you can use in one session—plus food coloring (This "ink" is washable. However, the more food coloring you add, the harder it is to wash out.)
  - The food finger paint recipe given earlier in this chapter: flour, water, and food coloring (See *Food Finger Paints, Variations*.)
  - Pudding or fruit-flavored gelatin (Before using either, let it stand at room temperature to soften.)

- A small plastic container (such as a margarine tub) or just the lid
- Paper towels
- Objects to use as stamps, such as:

  - Store-bought stamps
  - Building blocks or ABC blocks with raised letters and pictures

- ❑ Spools
- ❑ Hair curlers
- ❑ A potato or a piece of soft wood with lines or a pattern cut into it
- ❑ Rubber puzzle pieces
- ❑ Cotton swabs (with adult supervision)
- ❑ The eraser on the end of a pencil (with adult supervision)
- ❑ Sponges cut into shapes

Safety note: Children who are still teething or who put objects in their mouths will need close supervision when playing with sponges because they may bite off pieces.

○ Paper, such as newsprint, paper bags, or paper towels

ACTIVITY

Pour some of the "ink" mixture into the plastic container or lid. Fold up a half sheet of paper towel and immerse it in the "ink." Then show your child how to press the stamp into the "ink" and how to use the stamp to make impressions on a piece of paper. (Tape the paper to the play surface so that it doesn't move around.) Point out that unless you dip the stamp again, the image gets lighter each time you use the stamp. Also show your child how to make handprints, fingerprints, and even footprints.

VARIATION

Give your toddler a container of ink made from water and food coloring along with a paint brush. (A 1-inch or 1½-inch brush works well.) Let your child paint the sidewalk. This type of ink leaves a light impression that eventually washes away. For indoor play, you might let your child paint the basement floor.

Purpose

For information on the benefits of this type of play, see the section entitled *Purpose* at the beginning of this chapter.

Things to Talk About

Some things to discuss as your child plays with ink are:

○ Shapes: "The round block made a round dot on the paper. Where else on your paper is there a round dot?"
○ Colors: "What colors did you use?" "Did you mix the colors to get a new one?"
○ Letters: "Look, there's a 'B.' That's the letter your name starts with." (With children of this age, it's best to just point out the letters in passing rather than emphasize them.)
○ Numbers: "Can you make three of these?" "Can you make a family of cats? Let's make four."
○ The impressions: "Did the stamp come out dark? Did you have to press hard on the paper towel to make it that dark?"
○ Spatial concepts: "Where did you make the stamps? At the top of the paper, the bottom, the sides?"
○ Fingerprints: "Your finger made its own design of swirls. When you make lots of fingerprints, they look like polka dots."

With this type of activity, where there's an end product, encourage your toddler to be proud of what he/she produced. Some things you might say to your child are: "Did you like what you did?" "Let's show Daddy (Mommy)." "Let's put it up on the refrigerator."

Homemade
Bubbles

For information on making your own bubble solution and on bubble play, see the chapter *Visual Tracking Toys and Activities*.

Fill and Dump Activities

Overview

Because children love messy activities, they truly enjoy fill and dump play. Often starting as early as 12 to 15 months of age, toddlers fill their toys and play containers with materials such as blocks, water, sand, or grain and watch what happens when they dump out the contents. This type of play is a tactile experience. It lets children explore with their fingers and move materials around in dramatic ways.

Purpose

Much of fill and dump play involves aiming and watching material move from one container to another. These activities are good for developing the following:

○ Eye-hand coordination
○ Finger dexterity
○ Visual tracking

In addition, fill and dump activities provide children with sensory stimulation and help them learn about gravity, volume, quantity, and cause and effect. Children also become aware of sequence—in order to empty a container, they must first fill it.

Ideas for Things to Do:

○ Solid Object Fill and Dump Activities
○ Dry Fill and Dump Activities
○ Wet Fill and Dump Activities

The instructions for these activities follow.

Solid Object Fill and Dump Activities

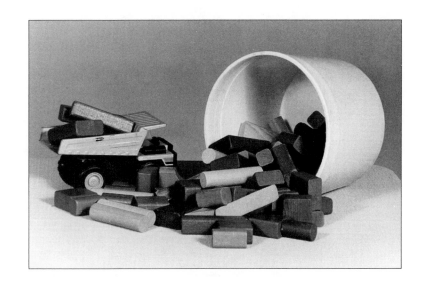

ACTIVITY

Have your child do any of the following:

○ Dump out the contents of a container, such as a coffee can, plastic storage container, carton, or box, that has been filled with blocks, spools, curlers, large beads, or other solid objects.

> **Safety note:** If you use a coffee can, pound down the inside rim to avoid sharp edges.

You can also use the size- and shape-sorting containers and objects described in the chapter *Stacking, Sorting, and Nesting Toys*. A milk or juice carton works especially well because it allows children to use the spout to pour out the objects instead of taking off the lid to remove them. Some toddlers enjoy this activity more if they can see the solid objects through a clear plastic container. Others prefer using a coffee can because of the sound the objects make when they hit the bottom.

○ Pour a variety of solid objects into a large container, such as a wash basin or box, and stir the objects with a large spoon.

○ Load blocks, curlers, or other solid objects into a toy dump truck or small wagon and then dump them out. (You can make a "wagon" by attaching a piece of rope to one side of a cardboard box. Your child can then pull the box around by its handle.)

○ Serve his/her own dry breakfast cereal by pouring it from a plastic bottle. The bottle should have a fairly wide opening and a handle (such as a plastic syrup bottle). You can remove the label to make the contents of the bottle more visible.

○ Empty a tall spice jar that's been filled with either an old telephone cord or the coil from a jogger's key ring. (A jogger's key ring has a clasp at one end, a ring at the other, and a tight brightly-colored plastic coil connecting them. For this activity, cut off the clasp and ring and use only the coil.)

> ***Safety note:*** Children need close supervision when playing with a telephone cord. A cord or rope longer than one foot can cause strangulation.

○ Place round objects into clear plastic bottles using the thumb and index finger. The round objects can be the lids from juice containers or plastic tops from milk jugs, and the plastic bottles should have wide openings, such as large pill bottles or spice jars. The bottles should also be short to avoid exceeding a toddler's attention span. (This activity is more challenging than any of the others listed here because it takes precise finger dexterity to fit the objects into the containers. Therefore, the activity is best suited to older toddlers.)

THINGS TO TALK ABOUT

As your child is filling and dumping solid objects, some things to discuss are:

○ The number of objects placed in a container: "You put one block into the bucket. You put two blocks . . ."

○ The color, size, or shape of the solid objects

○ Sounds: "The block made a big bang when you dropped it into the can." "What kind of noise did you hear when you dumped everything out of the container?"

○ Volume: "The container is full."

○ The child's actions: "Could you just drop things in the container, or did you have to push them through the opening?" "Did things pour out of the container, or did you have to reach in and pull them out?"

○ Pretend play: "Are you stirring a pot of soup? What's in it?"

Dry Fill
and Dump
Activities

WHAT YOU'LL NEED

○ Any of the following materials:

❑ Sand (for children who no longer put things in their mouths)
❑ Pasta. The different shapes and colors of pasta make it interesting for children. You can also add color to it in the following way:

△ Put a few drops of food coloring in a plastic bag.
△ Fill the bag half way with pasta, close it, and shake it.
△ Spread out the pasta on a cookie sheet and place it in an oven set at a very low temperature to dry out. (You can put it in an oven that's been turned off after baking.)

Safety note: Because dry pasta does not soften in the mouth and can cause choking, it's suitable only for older children who no longer put things in their mouths

❑ Dry cereal or grain, such as oatmeal, cornmeal, or rice (available in large quantities, such as 20-pound bags). You can color rice the same way you color pasta, by following the steps described on the previous page.

Safety note: Avoid using beans since children can easily choke on them or put them in their ears or nose.

❑ Wild birdseed (millet). Choose a birdseed that contains no sunflower seeds, which can be difficult for a child to swallow. (With birdseed, there's no waste. If it's spilled outside, the birds will eat it; and if it's spilled inside, you can sweep it up and toss it outside for the birds.)

○ A large container, such as a plastic wash basin, baby bathtub, cake pan with a sliding lid, or a tote (a rubber or plastic container with handles and a snug-fitting lid). Containers with lids work well for storing the fill and dump material for future use.

○ A sheet or tablecloth (Cleaning up is easier with a fabric covering than with plastic because dry fill and dump materials tend to bounce or slide off of plastic during play. Also, plastic is stiff and harder to aim and control when you're trying to pour the spilled material back into the container.)

ACTIVITY

Spread out the sheet or tablecloth on the floor. Place the container on top and fill it halfway with the fill and dump material. Give your child toys such as the following to play with:

○ A small dump truck and bulldozer
○ Small sand toys, such as a shovel with a short handle and a rake
○ Nesting toys, such as nesting cups
○ Kitchen items, such as measuring spoons and cups, an ice cream scooper, a mixing spoon, a scoop (the type used to remove flour from a canister), and a funnel with a large opening.

Two ways to make a funnel are:

❑ Using a small bleach bottle, remove the cap and rinse out the bottle. With a utility knife or scissors, cut off the bottom of the bottle about an inch below the handle.
❑ Using a clear plastic syrup bottle, remove the label and cap and cut off the bottom, leaving most of the bottle intact.

○ A teacup set or toy cooking and eating utensils.
○ A gravity wheel (also called water wheel or sand wheel). Make sure the hole is large enough for dry materials to flow through.
○ A piece of hose or clear flexible vinyl tubing, about 1 inch in diameter and about 10 to 12 inches long. Children enjoy filling the tube and watching the material flow out the bottom.
○ Cylinder-shaped plastic containers, such as pill bottles. Drill holes in them—a large hole in the bottom of one container and several small holes in the bottom of another. Have your toddler fill the containers and watch how fast or slowly the material pours out of each. Point out that the size and number of holes make the difference.

It's a good idea to group toys and to introduce them together on separate occasions instead of offering your child a variety of unrelated toys. Grouping toys by type, such as cooking and eating utensils, enhances a child's learning experience by demonstrating how certain toys are related. It also encourages imaginative, creative play.

Also remember that children enjoy a change in toys. Periodically substituting one set of fill and dump toys with another changes children's focus and keeps their interest level and attention span high.

To clean up after fill and dump play, put all of the toys in the tub. Then brush off your child over the sheet. Next, remove the tub, gather up the sheet to form a funnel, and pour the fill and dump material back into the container. Then cover and store the material for next time. Children usually enjoy using a small hand-held vacuum cleaner to help do the final cleanup.

THINGS TO TALK ABOUT

As your child is filling and dumping dry materials, some things to discuss are:

○ Textures (since each material has its own feel): "The birdseed is silky." "The oatmeal feels scratchy."

○ Volume: "You filled this container to the top." "Now that container is empty." "Will the rice from this cup fill up the bigger cup?" "Which opening lets the oatmeal come through faster—the big one or the small one?"

○ Size: "Which of these containers is bigger?"

○ Directions: "You poured the birdseed in the top of the tube, and it's coming out the bottom."

○ Shapes and colors: "Look at the different colors of pasta. Can you find the blue circle?"

○ Cause and effect: "Look what happens when I put my hand over the hole. The cereal stops falling."

○ Pretend play: "Let's pretend to have lunch. Can you pour the make-believe milk into my cup?" "Is it hard to drive your truck through the rice?"

Wet Fill and Dump Activities

WHAT YOU'LL NEED

- For outside play, a wading pool
- For inside play, a large container (any of those listed for dry fill and dump activities) and a sheet of plastic, such as an old shower curtain or tablecloth, to place under it (Another alternative is to make wet fill and dump play a bathtub activity.)

ACTIVITY

If you're using a container, spread out the plastic on the floor and place the plastic container on top of it. Fill it halfway with warm water. Otherwise, put your toddler in the wading pool or bathtub. Give your child the same toys described earlier in this chapter for the dry fill and dump activities plus:

- Bathtub blocks
- Boats, either purchased or made from the following:

  - Bathtub blocks or sponges cut into a boat shape with an electric carving knife or other sharp knife. (To make cutting easier, make the sponges stiff by first wetting them and then letting them dry.) For a mast, stick a tongue depressor or Popsicle stick in the middle of the sponge. Cut a sail from a plastic milk jug or a plastic report cover and attach the sail by cutting two holes or slits in the plastic with scissors and threading the plastic onto the mast.

> *Safety note:* Because they may bite off pieces, children who are still teething or who put objects in their mouths will need close supervision when playing with sponges or bathtub blocks.

❑ Scraps of wood. Use contact cement to glue a mast made from a short, narrow piece of dowel rod to wood scrap boat. Make and attach a sail following the preceding set of instructions.

> *Safety note:* Because of chemicals, avoid using scraps cut from pressure-treated lumber.

○ Wooden shapes from other activities, such as blocks and spools
○ Kitchen utensils, such as a baster, plastic bowls, funnel, and hand egg beater (especially fun when bubbles are in the water and an adult beats it)
○ A toy sprinkling can or large plastic spice bottle with a shaker lid (Rinse it out and remove the label.)
○ Small squeeze bottles
○ Balls

> *Safety note:* Children who are still teething or who put objects in their mouths will need close supervision when playing with foam or rubber balls because they may bite off pieces. Foam balls are especially dangerous because they're very soft and easy for children to squeeze and bite.

○ A water wheel. The height of the wheel will determine the depth of the water in the tub or pool unless you place the wheel on top of an object. A plastic storage crate turned upside down makes a stable base.

○ Soap crayons

○ Bubbles, scents (such as extracts or cologne), or a small amount of food coloring. While children enjoy these additions to the water, you need to watch out for allergic reactions. To minimize the chance of a reaction, it's best to introduce small amounts of these items when your child is playing in a dish pan of water rather than a pool or bathtub.

○ A doll. For boys as well as girls a doll is useful for modeling safe behavior in the water. For example, you can use the doll to demonstrate the idea of sitting upright in the water. Children also enjoy using the doll in pretend play activities—giving the doll a bath and washing its hair.

○ A large chunk of ice. Fill a container with water, add some food coloring (so that the ice doesn't blend in with the water), and freeze it. Remove the ice from the container and place it in the water. Children can watch the ice float, try to pick it up, balance objects on top of it, and watch it as it gets smaller and smaller.

The same recommendations made for dry fill and dump activities (grouping toys and changing them periodically) apply here as well. See that portion of this chapter for additional information.

Things to Talk About

Some things to discuss while your child is involved in wet fill and dump activities are:

○ Gravity: "What happened when we had a hole in the bottom of the container? Where did the water go?"

○ Velocity: "When there's a little hole in the container, the water pours out slowly. When there's a big hole, the water pours out fast. What happens when there are lots of little holes?"

○ Size: "Which bucket has more water?"

○ Weight: "When you dropped the sponge in the water, did it make a big splash? What happened when you dropped the block?"

○ Buoyancy: "Let's see if this toy will float or sink."
○ Volume: "This container is full; that one is empty." "You poured the water to the top of the cup."
○ Directions: "You poured the water down the spout, and it came out the bottom."
○ Cause and effect: "Let's see what happens when you pour the water onto the water wheel."
○ Pretend play: "This sponge is a boat, and this spool is a person. The boat chugs along and stops to pick up the person." "Let's give this baby a bath."

If your child is playing with ice in the water, you can also discuss how cold it feels, how it floats, what happens when it melts, and what color it is. If your child is playing with bathtub blocks, you can discuss how they stick to each other and to the side of the tub and how you can stack them. With sponges, you can talk about stacking them and about how squeezing them makes the sponges lighter.

Books

Overview

Most children love books from an early age. By the time they are 12 to 18 months old, toddlers enjoy both looking at the pictures and talking about them.

Toddler books are usually sturdy and short. Six to eight pages is a good length because a toddler's attention span for "reading" books is only about two to five minutes. Among the topics usually covered in toddler books are animals, nursery rhymes, numbers, the alphabet, and families.

If your child has special interests, it may be hard to find books that fit those interests and are appropriate to your child's age. A solution to this problem is to make your own books. This chapter describes three types of books you can make to match your child's interests and readiness. Among the topics you can cover in homemade books are:

○ Your child—Include baby pictures along with current snapshots of your child doing things throughout the day, such as eating, napping, taking a bath, and playing. Also add photographs of your house, pets, your child's security object, and family members. It's a good idea to include relatives who live far away to help your child become familiar with them. Having a book about themselves helps children develop their identity. It gives them a perspective (though limited) on who they are and how they've grown.

- ○ Toys
- ○ Stuffed animals
- ○ Dolls
- ○ Cars, trucks, and trains
- ○ Earthmoving equipment
- ○ Textures—Use a different piece of textured fabric or other object (such as a leaf or feather) on each page.
- ○ Foods
- ○ Colors
- ○ Nursery rhyme characters
- ○ Familiar objects—You might include items such as a cup, spoon, window, and bathtub.
- ○ Opposites—Place the opposites on facing pages to show contrast, such as something tall and something short, or something light and something dark.
- ○ Numbers—For this age group, show only the numbers one through four.
- ○ Animals—Toddlers enjoy seeing pictures of mother and baby animals, zoo animals, and farm animals.
- ○ Occupations—Show pictures of people performing their jobs, such as a police officer, fire fighter, mail carrier, and doctor.
- ○ Clothes—Illustrate different seasons by showing a raincoat, mittens, sandals, etc.
- ○ Places—Include various places your child visits, such as church, the library, the grocery store, and the park.
- ○ A vacation or outing

Recommendations

Illustrate your books with photographs, drawings, stickers, or pictures from coloring books. If the coloring-book pictures are too large, use a photocopying machine to reduce them to a smaller size before coloring them.

Other sources for pictures are postcards, greeting cards, catalogs, and magazines. For hard-to-find pictures, contact companies related to the topic. For example, by contacting an engineering company you might be able to get old copies of trade publications, catalogs, and annual reports that have pictures of earthmoving equipment.

Purpose

Reading books aloud and discussing the pictures with children can do the following:

○ Help children develop a love of books and an interest in reading
○ Broaden their vocabulary, giving them words to think and communicate with
○ Provide them with simple early reading experiences if you label the pictures in the books you make (appropriate as children get older)

Reading books can also benefit children's physical development. Turning the pages of a book requires crossing the midline—body control that involves reaching and grasping across the midline of the body.

Things to Talk About

As you look at books with your child, ask questions about the pictures: "What colors are all of the things on this page?" "Which picture is bigger?" "Who delivers our mail?" "Where do we go to buy shoes?"

Tell stories, recite rhymes, or sing songs about the pictures. For example, you might sing "Old MacDonald" as you look through an animal book. Children especially like it when you personalize the songs or rhymes by using their names. You could substitute your child's name for Mary in "Mary Had a Little Lamb."

In time your toddler will become very familiar with the books you've made. You can then ask your child to make up one or two sentences about each of the pictures they contain. Write the sentences on each page. Later, read them back, telling your child his/her very own story.

Books You Can Make:

○ Album Books
○ Lunch Bag Books
○ Folder Books

The instructions for making these books follow.

Album Books

WHAT YOU'LL NEED

○ A small hand-held photo album, such as a commercially available parent's or grandparent's brag book
○ Pictures small enough to fit in the album
○ Tape

STEPS TO FOLLOW

1. Insert the pictures in the album.
2. Place a small piece of tape over the opening where you inserted the picture.

ACTIVITY

Help your toddler turn the pages of the book and discuss the pictures with him/her.

THINGS TO TALK ABOUT

See the beginning of this chapter.

Lunch Bag Books

WHAT YOU'LL NEED

○ Index cards (4 × 6 inches) or a piece of posterboard cut into pieces that will fit into the plastic bags
○ Pictures no larger than the index or posterboard cards
○ Rubber cement
○ Resealable plastic storage bags
○ Two metal notebook rings

STEPS TO FOLLOW

1. Use rubber cement to glue the pictures onto each side of an index or posterboard card.
2. Place each card into a resealable plastic bag and seal the bag. If your child is teething, be sure the card completely fills the corners of the bag.
3. Stack the bags with each of the resealable edges on the left.
4. Attach the plastic bags together using the two metal notebook rings. Poke one ring through the upper portion of each bag and one ring through the lower portion. Position the rings just to the right of the resealable edge.

ACTIVITY

Help your toddler turn the pages of the book and discuss the pictures with him/her.

VARIATION

Remove the pages of the book to play a matching game. For example, you might take out pictures of household objects, such as a television set and a couch. Give these pictures to your child and ask him/her to find the objects in the house. (Matching is a skill that prepares toddlers for later reading. In developing this skill, children are learning to visually discriminate—identifying similarities and differences, making comparisons, and mentally grouping and associating objects.)

Occasionally test your toddler's perception skills by handing the picture to the child upside down. See if he/she turns it right-side up.

THINGS TO TALK ABOUT

See the beginning of this chapter.

Folder Books

WHAT YOU'LL NEED

- Two to three manila folders (Either buy folders with straight edges or cut off the tabs.)
- Pictures large enough to cover each side of the folders
- Rubber cement
- Clear adhesive paper
- A permanent marker or ballpoint pen
- A hole punch
- Two metal notebook rings

STEPS TO FOLLOW

1. Use rubber cement to glue the pictures onto both the inside and outside surfaces of each folder.
2. Cover the pictures with clear adhesive paper extending to the folder's edges.
3. Stack the folders with the open sides on the right. Mark two holes along the left side of each folder, positioning the holes about 2 inches from the top and 2 inches from the bottom.

4. Use a hole punch to make the holes.
5. Attach all of the folders together using the two metal notebook rings. (If you choose, you can attach the folders by tying them with string or ribbon. However, tying puts stress on the holes, making them more likely to tear over time.)

ACTIVITY

Help your toddler turn the pages of the book and discuss the pictures with him/her.

THINGS TO TALK ABOUT

See the beginning of this chapter.

GLOSSARY

Anticipation	looking forward to an event based on previous experience
Body awareness	knowledge of body parts: where each part is, what it does, how it might feel, and how it relates to the rest of the body
Cause and effect	the relationship between an event or action and an outcome
Color perception	seeing and understanding the physical characteristics of colors and the differences between them
Coordination	the ability of parts of the body to work together smoothly to perform actions
Crossing the midline	body control that involves reaching and grasping across the midsection of the body without moving other parts of the body (for example, reaching across the body with the right arm without moving the left arm or twisting the head or trunk)

Directionality	an awareness of the placement of objects in relation to one's body (above, below, in front of, behind, to the left or right)
Eye-hand coordination	the ability of the eyes and hands to work together smoothly to accomplish a task
Fine motor skill	the ability to control and coordinate the movements of the small muscles, those of the eyes, hands, feet, fingers, and toes; the skill needed to carry out activities such as grasping and stacking blocks (also called *small motor skill*)
Finger dexterity	the ease, skill, and speed with which the fingers carry out physical activity
Generalizing	inferring a general concept from particular pieces of information
Goal setting	the ability to establish an end result and work to achieve it
Gross motor skill	the ability to control and coordinate the movements of the large muscles, those of the trunk, arms, and legs; the skill needed to carry out activities such as climbing, throwing, and running (also called *large motor skill*)
Long-distance eye-hand coordination	the ability of the eyes and hands to work together to perform a gross motor skill a distance from the body, such as tossing, catching, and hitting a ball
Manipulative play	using the hands and fingers to handle or rearrange play materials
One-to-one correspondence	matching one object to another
Patterning skills	the ability to identify patterns or arrangements of parts that make up a whole, such as the letters that make up a word

Pre-reading activities	activities that prepare a child physically and mentally to learn to read
Pretend play	play in which a child creates imaginary objects, people, and/or events (also called *imaginative play*)
Problem solving	identifying the means to achieve an end result
Readiness	preparedness to learn based on biological maturation and experience with concepts and materials
Sense of balance	the ability to keep the position of the body steady in relation to gravity and while muscles interact
Sensory stimulation	anything that causes messages to be sent from the senses to the brain
Shape perception	seeing and understanding the physical characteristics of individual shapes
Size perception	seeing and understanding the amount of space something occupies; an awareness of the dimensions and magnitude of an object or image
Spatial awareness	an understanding of where objects are in relation to one another or to one's self (for example, on top of, next to, inside, below)
Two-hand coordination	the ability of the hands to work together smoothly to accomplish a task, such as holding an object steady with one hand and hammering it with the other
Visual discrimination	the ability to see how images are the same and different
Visual tracking	the ability of the eye muscles to work together to follow an object through space (also called *eye tracking*)
Whole body control	the ability to coordinate the movement of the trunk and limbs to complete a task

INDEX